[redacted]

MORRIS VAHNI[redacted]

The Road to Real Estate Wealth

Secrets to Success in Any Market

11/20/12

To: Comfort Cheng

Thank for purchasing my Book. Enjoy the Book. Go get them!!

M V

Special discounts on bulk quantities of The Road to Real Estate Wealth Publishing books are available to corporations, professional associations, and other organizations. For details, contact Special Sales Department, The Road to Real Estate Publishing, an imprint of Road to Real Estate Wealth Publications, a division of

The Road to Real Estate Worth, LLC,
20533 Biscayne Blvd suite 263
Aventura FL 33180
Fax 954-239-9640

Printed in the United States of America.
by ECPrinting.com
Eau Claire, WI
1-888-832-1135

20533 Biscayne Blvd suite 263
Aventura FL 33180

ISBN: 978-1-4276-3471-9

I want to thank my dear wife for being my inspiration and my partner in life. I also want to thank those who helped me along my journey of success.

Why I Chose to Write This Book

When I decided that I wanted to be a professional real estate investor, I was still a senior in college. I was months from graduation, anxiously and nervously preparing myself to go out into the world. I started out in this business with no money, few skills, and scant genuine knowledge. The difference between calling myself a real estate investor and actually *being* an investor was a feat that took time and involved overcoming many obstacles. It was nearly two years before I actually broke the ice and completed my first deal. You see, wanting to do something and actually doing it are two very different things. An obvious point? Perhaps, but such understanding and living such seemingly mundane issues are the stuff that separate those who accomplish from those who still only wish to excel. Many people are, as I was, full of fear and ignorance, and those two things can stop anyone from breaking out and taking control of his or her life.

From the time I decided to learn as much as I could about the real estate business, I read voraciously and took as many courses as I could get my hands on. Once I started to experience success, I realized that most courses and books are laden with theoretical musings but offer minimal real, practical knowledge of the sort that potential investors can put to profitable use. About five years ago, I decided that somewhere down the road I would write a book that would highlight my own experience and real-life practices. I wanted to eliminate all the "guru" fluff. I wanted to write a book that would help flatten the learning curve of anyone ambitious enough to make it in the world of real estate investing. Everything that I teach and talk about in this book comes from experience and encompasses what I have actually done.

Contents

Part Three

Where It All Began: Moe's Story

As I write this, I am 34 years old and have already bought and sold nearly 400 properties, including a 56-unit building and a 65-unit mobile home park. I currently own and manage a 66-unit apartment building and 100 single-family homes as part of my long-term real estate holdings.

I was born in Jerusalem in 1973. My parents emigrated from Morocco to Israel in the '50s, where they met and married. I am an only child, yet was born into a large family of many cousins and aunts and uncles, most of whom still reside abroad. I had a normal upbringing, but our family just got by financially. Budgets were tight and not always met. When I was nine years old, my parents decided to take my uncle's advice and move to the land of opportunity: the United States of America.

Even as a nine-year-old kid, I was extremely excited. To children, especially back then, America represented opportunity; perhaps most important, it was the home of Disneyland! We boarded a jet one morning, landed at JFK in New York, and then drove to Philadelphia, where a friend's family took us in.

I feel I came to United States at an ideal age. At the age of nine, you may have many friends, but you remain flexible about change, and have yet to build the long-term bonds of friendship that come during your teen years. Don't get me wrong; any transition into a different culture at any age is a challenge. But coming here at such a young age helped me to smoothly transition into and understand the way of life here in America.

Most of my family, including my parents, did not have a

college education. Some had no high school education. This meant that they had to rely on blue-collar work to make a living. My dad worked as a paper hanger, and my mom was a hairstylist. Although I believe school is not the secret to success, it can help a person learn to think. Of course, many successful people never finished high school, and some self-taught educators have never been to college but are very bright. My parents were hard-working immigrants who did what they knew, and what society had taught them to do.

The first few months in America were difficult. I was trying to fit into a new culture while trying to strengthen my language skills. I tried my hardest to be as outgoing and friendly as possible. We lived with our friend's family for the first year, after which we were finally able to get our own place. This was the first time in my life that I actually had my own room! You see, apartments abroad are for the most part smaller than in the States. Here, finally, I got my own room. Over the next few years, I acclimated to this way of life and made new friends, including one friend I'm still very close to.

As I entered high school, my thoughts turned toward my future. Money was a big topic in my home throughout my upbringing, or should I say the lack of money. I think this constant issue of not having much money planted a subconscious seed in my mind that urged me to do whatever it took to have enough resources so I would not have to worry about paying my bills. I think that made me a driven young man with lots of dreams and ambition. I was a very average student in school, perhaps because I kept highlighting my work with a black marker! Language was a constant issue and a constant struggle. My work habits were not yet my strength. Being an only child and having both parents working hard all the time meant I did not have anyone constantly watching over me. Having a lot of freedom like this can be often unfavorable for teenagers, but I think for me this environment helped me become more mature. When I was a high school freshman, the majority of my friends were seniors—not very common. I think my sophomore year was a pivotal year for me. I loved sports and considered myself a good athlete, but I got caught up in the social scene of high school, and did not participate in after-school activities to a great degree. Not having the best grades and not having the authority to control my destiny, I felt that being involved with after-school activities would help me become more involved in school itself. So I made a commitment to get involved with after-school activities and sports. I reasoned that this would help me improve my grades and give me an opportunity to later play in college, perhaps even earn a scholarship.

In my junior year, I joined the high school soccer team. I was good at soccer, and this skill improved my social association with other students. This, in turn, helped me get back on track and kept me socially grounded.

I had great junior year and improved my grades. We took a trip as a team during my junior year: four days in Fort Lauderdale for a tournament against teams from around the country. We held a fundraiser to help pay for the trip and then we were off. That was the first time I went to South Florida (now my home). I have to admit I felt very comfortable in Florida and fell in love with the area. For some crazy reason, even as a 17-year-old, I knew that one day I would be back. I don't know why. It's just something I felt, and I remember it like it was yesterday. I even mentioned it to my teammates.

I continued that momentum into my senior year: I had a great soccer season, and my academic work improved considerably. I even started to highlight my workbook with a normal neon-yellow highlighter. I was an all-state soccer player and Player of the Year. I received a handful of awards, but most importantly, I generated interest from college soccer scouts. The award I am most proud of was given "for the player who gave of himself for the betterment of the team." That award summed up what I was, and am, about. I feel that team sports help build a person's character and leadership skills. I was hoping to use my skills and my soccer to help myself get into a good college and jump-start my education at a higher level. I spent the second half of my senior year driving around to different universities, talking to department heads and soccer coaches. I visited a multitude of universities from upstate New York all the way to the Carolinas. Those were good times: getting in the car, taking a road trip with buddies, and looking at the future. I even remember being told by university representatives that they thought I would succeed anywhere I went.

This was a great compliment and quite a confidence booster.

I chose to go to Penn State University, which I attended in the fall of 1992. I knew college work was going to be a challenge since I had been only an average student in high school. I knew I had to step up my study time and improve my discipline. After the first semester, I took a trip with a friend from Pennsylvania to South Florida. We spent a month in my first car, a 1972 Superbug Beetle, which I bought for $1,000. Let me tell you, driving a Beetle on the highway means you will never fall asleep at the wheel, and you will never get a speeding ticket. It's quite an experience; every time I coughed, the windshield fogged up. My knees nearly touched my chin as I drove. It was definitely not a ride of luxury. But I spent a good amount of time in South Florida and really got a feel for what the place was like. We did not have much money, and to extend our trip, we hooked up with a few family friends who helped us get odd jobs during our stay.

After heading home, I really felt a desire to move permanently to Florida. Since my parents were living from paycheck to paycheck, and were not business owners or home owners, they had no real financial ties to Philadelphia. I thought it would be a great idea for them to move down to South Florida. Since they had a few friends from Philadelphia who had made the move to South Florida, it was a much easier sale. To my surprise, my enthusiasm and excitement rubbed off on them, and within a matter of months they made the move. Since I had just started my first year of college, my initial thought was to stay put and finish school. But after my second semester (and living in my uncle's basement), I decided to transfer to South Florida.

Once again, my parents were living in a one-bedroom rented apartment. I moved in with them. I chose to go to a local community college for that first year. During many late-night television viewings, I remember watching a local cable television channel that strictly televised real estate for sale. Local investors and Realtors purchased time and displayed their inventory for sale. For some crazy reason, I enjoyed watching it. Now, I majored in business in college. I was definitely not an engineer or an architect or anything technical. I certainly wasn't smart enough for these disciplines. I was a solid "C" student. I knew nothing about real estate, but for some reason, I enjoyed watching hours of the real estate channel. Watching that channel, I realized that I was intensely interested in real estate.

I worked really hard that year in community college. I busted my hump to stay on track and not lose any time in the transition. Once again, this was a new environment with new people and a new system, but I persevered. I graduated from Miami-Dade Community College with a two-year associate degree in business and transferred to Florida Atlantic University in Boca Raton, Florida. And, for the first time in my life, I moved out of my parents' home and lived on campus.

I was able to play soccer at the university and continued to work hard in school. My grades stayed pretty constant—just as in high school. Toward the end of my junior year, someone introduced me to a multi-level marketing business. Even though the business wasn't for me, the experience and knowledge that I gained definitely helped me grow as a person and helped me define myself. To become successful in that business, you must first become a good leader. So I studied the principles of success and what it takes to be a fine leader. I became a student of success. I read dozens of books on self-improvement and dealing with people. I also listened to hundreds of cassette tapes from people who had been successful in the corporate world, but now yearned to get out of the rat race and find something better. You see, real estate is all about financial freedom and taking control of your own time. I liked the idea of the lifestyle that they were describing. This learning experience was the step that I needed to change my mindset. Now I had started to transform my thought processes.

The way you think is a very important first step toward success in any business, but especially in real estate. Unfortunately, they don't teach college students how to be successful through achieving financial freedom.

I was a 21-year-old college student with everything in front of me. I had a thirst and hunger for knowledge. I drove 12 hours one way for a weekend seminar. I invested in the most important muscle in my body, my brain. This experience helped me grow as a person. There seemed to be real differences now between me and the average 21-year-old college student. As I neared graduation, I knew I was getting closer to my crossroads: take a job with a guaranteed paycheck or take the entrepreneurial path that offered no guarantees but no limitations, either.

My last year in college, I moved off campus and rented an apartment with a roommate, like so many college students. And living in Florida has perks, what with great weather all year-round. During our leisure and stress-release times, we often headed outside and played tennis and basketball. During one game, I got to talking to a friend; I don't remember how we got to this, but I asked him how much he was spending on rent. He told me he owned his place, which was identical to my apartment. I thought that was kind of cool that he owned his own condo. I asked how much he paid for the condo. Based on that, I calculated a mortgage payment of $400 per month. I asked how much the condo fees were and was told they were $150. Now understand: I was renting an identical apartment for $800 a month, and the current owner was an out-of-state absentee owner who used a Realtor to manage the apartment—the same Realtor who rented us the apartment. So this absentee owner was making probably between $200 and $300 a month in positive cash flow, plus his tax deduction, plus building equity, and all with very little work.

This just made sense to me, and it clicked in my mind. And, coming off my previous business venture (multi-level marketing), I was trying to become involved in something that would bring me financial independence and passive income. At that point, I viewed real estate as a vehicle that could give me that lifestyle. I can pinpoint this moment in my life. At that very moment, I decided I wanted to be a real estate investor. Shortly after that, I graduated from college.

That was in June of 1996. I did not have any interest in continuing my formal education at this point. I was motivated to just get out there and start making money. I graduated with a degree in business and a major in finance. Of course, having a lot of dreams and hopes and ambition is one thing, but having financial resources is another. During my whole college career, I worked as a waiter in various restaurants. I got through with the help of my parents and my temporary jobs, just like most other students. My parents were amazing people who helped me as best they could. I knew I wanted to be a real estate investor, but I soon realized that it was much harder than I had at first thought it would be, having no money, no job, and no experience. So I had to find a job. I sent my résumé to hundreds of places. I was over-educated for many entry-level positions and under-qualified due to having zero experience in the real world. I found myself working at temp agencies and doing odd jobs just to get by.

One thing I did maintain was good credit, and that paid off soon enough. I got licensed to sell life insurance and worked for a brief period of time at John Hancock Life Insurance in Miami. But I did not have a passion for it.

I decided not sit around and wait for something to develop. I was still very much in the hunt to learn about real estate and find a way to do my first deal. I got my real estate salesperson license and continued to look at properties, take courses, and purchase books, tapes, and courses from infomercials. I was not sitting on my hands. I had to do what I had to do to pay my bills, but I was simultaneously educating myself and learning the business of real estate, and banging my head against the wall trying to bridge the gap between talking about being a real estate investor and actually doing it. And I learned what I believe separates a very successful person from an ordinary person:

1. What you do when you're not working.
2. Who your friends are.
3. How you think.

I became a student of success. I understood the principles of success, and I was using those principles and applying them toward my goals.

To stay focused, I used props to keep me on track; I wrote what I wanted to accomplish and printed it up and put it on my wall so I could look at it every day. It may sound cheesy, but life is full of pitfalls, and you need to stay focused on your own path. You have to tell yourself what you want and convince your subconscious mind what it is that you need to accomplish. You need to picture what you want before you have it. Even though I did not yet fully understand a lot of the techniques I was using for success, I trusted the people who taught me these skills and took a leap of faith.

The year after graduation was a vitally important time in my life. Which path would I take? Could I to stick to real estate and the uncertainty that would lie ahead? Or would I settle for a nine-to-five desk job with a salary? During this time, I bounced from job to job, but I did not take my eyes off what I really wanted, and that was to become involved in real estate. I also knew I wanted to be a principal, not an agent. There is nothing wrong with being a real estate agent, but that wasn't what I was attracted to; I wanted to own, not broker, real estate. I got my agent's license so I would be armed with additional knowledge and tools.

I tried many things in my quest to purchase. Of course, having no money, I was constantly trying to use "creative financing." I was attempting to get the sellers to go for every creative financing technique I had learned. (I think a seller would have had to have been Houdini to make a deal work for me. I tried working probate, I tried working with HUD, I tried making offers to "for sale by owners," and I tried contacting other agents. Basically, I tried any way to get involved. Not having any money wasn't helping. Also, one thing that took some time to overcome was *fear*. I probably could have purchased a deal along the way, but perhaps that fear stopped me.)

One of the courses that I had purchased preached that potential investors should obtain as many credit cards as possible. I realized that, without owning any real estate that I could borrow against, credit cards offered the only way to borrow money based on my signature alone. So I sat down one day, from nine to five, and applied for as many credit cards as I could. Believe it or not, I eventually developed $33,000 worth of cash advance credit to my name.

Using the skills I had learned in another course and trial and error (where I learned to recognize a potential deal through the specific wording of an advertisement), I stumbled onto an ad that attracted me. The ad said, "probate sale, purchase below market value." I called the number on the ad and learned that the property was a condo. Not only was it a nice two-bedroom, two-bath, fully furnished condo, but I could also picture myself living there. The condo was worth $55,000. I was able to purchase it for $30,000, which I was able to pay in cash from cash advances from the credit cards. But don't fool yourself, I did my homework. You see, real estate is not mere gambling; it is gambling with knowledge. I went to my local bank and found to my delight that they would give me 70% of the market value on a loan, which in this case was $38,000. I could purchase the property for $30,000 plus closing costs, and then refinance it with a mortgage and pay back the credit cards. So, not only could I purchase this property with no up-front cash, but I could pocket $6,000! That is exactly what I did. It all started with the purchase of one small apartment.

Everything started to come together after that. I had been able to break the ice and overcome my fear. The person I bought the property from was an investor who took me under his wing and helped me develop my business. Don't get me wrong—the work had just begun, but I was finally able to enjoy the feeling of actually purchasing a property and seeing results. I also realized that all the books and tapes had good information: you *can* purchase real estate with no money out of pocket. I also learned that having knowledge is just as important as having money. Money does make things easier, but having an understanding of how to recognize a deal and evaluate it is far more important. That revelation helped me develop a sense of confidence that I still hold to this day.

I would have to work harder than ever, but now I started to work smart, honing my ability and building my bank account. I learned how to put other people's efforts and skills to work for me. I became a real estate conductor, and my baton was my mobile phone. Through learning how to leverage my time through a network of people, I was able to realize my dream of being financially independent. I have offices in Tampa, Birmingham, and the South Florida area, where I have a real estate investment business. I am also buying and selling, and maintaining an active investment portfolio of more than 50 short-term properties. Once you learn the skills (and through this book I will teach you), you can apply them anywhere.

Married now for more than eight years, I have been blessed with three children, a five-year-old girl, a three-year-old boy, and a new baby girl.

My life is very exciting. I now don't have to worry about money; it's simply not an issue for me. I don't look at price tags when I shop. I live in a multimillion-dollar home. I drive top-of-the-line cars, and go on the best vacations every four months and belong to country clubs. Yet the most important things for me are not the materialistic things in life, but the lifestyle I enjoy and the freedom I have to spend time with my family and friends. I don't have a boss and never need to ask permission to take off with my family. Even before I started this business, I pictured myself having a family, and I wanted to be able to spend as much time with them as I could. Even before I got here, while still a college student, I listened to the success stories of individuals who already had families but were in the rut that can be corporate America. All they talked about was how they wanted to have control over their lives, and not have a boss over them telling them what to do. This, to me, is the most important aspect of success.

And now, 10 years later, I'm so happy that I stayed with it. I was persistent, and have been rewarded with a great lifestyle and complete control of my own life. I've never had a regular job in my adult life, and I'm not planning on it. We all have struggles that we need to overcome in order to succeed. Most of the struggles that people go through are built in their own minds through years of society telling them how to live, or because they sought advice from the wrong people. Success is definitely a journey, not a destination.

I am only 34 years old with still a lot of time in front of me. I am only getting started; I am constantly learning and growing, and am excited about what the future holds for me.

For more details about my entry into real estate, feel free to visit my website at www.TheRoadToRealEstateWealth.com.

Part One:
The Many Hats of the Real Estate Investor

As you progress through this book, you will be learning many things about a host of tasks directly and indirectly related to real estate. You will need to learn how to manage the resources and network of people who can help you with your quest for success and happiness. First and foremost: You are getting involved in a business, and you need to treat it like a business. Over the years, I have seen many people get involved in real estate and not treat it like a business. You need to be organized and aggressive, and, most importantly, work with people who are the same way.

For example, if you hire a real estate agent and he or she doesn't respect your time or won't work hard for you, then move on to someone else. Dedicated people will be one of your most important assets. Similarly, like any business owner, you must learn about inventory (the real estate you will own), bookkeeping (tracking your income and expenses), hiring (as your business grows), sales (to promote yourself and your properties), and a lot more. These areas represent many different job positions and descriptions. With one-owner, small businesses, the owner-operator spends time doing different jobs that, in a large company, would be assigned to different people. Thus, the owner must learn to wear different "hats" to keep his business running smoothly. Nonetheless, don't be intimidated by all this. You don't need to be an expert in every area of the business, because you can hire people to do much of it for you. Still, the variety of tasks you will take on is one of the things that makes running your own business fun—be it a real estate business or a restaurant or what have you—and so exciting. Most people are stuck doing one boring thing day-in and day-out at their jobs. Not so with a small-business owner.

To illustrate, let's examine another business, a humble hotdog stand. As the owner of a hotdog stand (don't laugh, hotdog stands can be very profitable in many cities), you may start by wearing your marketing hat and selecting a good location and choosing colorful signage so you can command attention from prospective customers. Then, it's time to put on the chef's hat and cook the hotdogs that you'll sell that day. That done, you may now picture yourself wearing the salesperson's hat to greet potential customers and convince them that your hotdogs are tastier than the competition's. Come evening, you don the bookkeeper's hat to tally up the day's sales and enter all the information into your ledger.

You see, the owner of a hotdog stand—itself just a compact,

freestanding restaurant—does not simply cook hot dogs. The owner must effectively change "hats" and perform different jobs, until and unless he decides to hire others to do these jobs for him. This changing of hats is often done subconsciously, but understand that it is best done with forethought and planning, and quite consciously. This is the most effective way to understand the jobs at hand and do them with gusto.

In my business as a real estate investor, I refer to the way I think about all of these tasks or job categories as the many "hats" of the investor. You will now learn what the person under each hat does, how he or she does it, and how to change hats at will, as needed, to make the most of your time and investment. I actually visualize what hat I will be wearing during a given day and time. I will lay it all out for you, and you can take whatever time you need to get comfortable with the information, because as you become an investor yourself, it will be you who must change hats when necessary.

Soon you, like any successful business owner, will be able to perform all the functions necessary to build real estate wealth. You'll feel comfortable doing each job, doing it well, and you won't end up feeling overwhelmed, something that often happens to those who don't capitalize on the experience of others (such as me) to lay out a clear path. You see, I am first and foremost an investor, and everything I will be sharing with you comes from experience.

Now let's take a look at each hat in turn:

1. The Investor Hat
2. The Appraiser Hat
3. The Contractor Hat
4. The Lawyer Hat
5. The Salesperson Hat
6. The Financing Hat
7. The Licensed Real Estate Agent Hat
8. The Motivational Hat
9. The Property Manager Hat

You will wear different hats at different times, but to illustrate the path to buying profitable properties, we will examine this in the usual order of a purchase. Ready? Let's get started!

The Investor Hat

As you probably guessed, the investor's tasks are among the most important for any real estate professional. Remember, this is a business, and you must treat it like one. For someone coming out of corporate America, single-minded focus is hard to overcome. Most of us are not exposed to a business in its totality. We generally participate in only a few areas or departments at most. But when you become an entrepreneur, you are everyone and everything. You are responsible for every aspect of management. Always try to stay business-oriented, learn all you can, and keep your emotions out of it.

First, here are a few key concepts to understand. When analyzing a potential investment property, you need to ask yourself these three questions:

1. What is the True Market Value? (variable)
2. What is the True Cost of Renovation?(variable)
3. What is the Price? (constant)

These three are areas you need to investigate and become adept at analyzing. The first two are variables, and accuracy in your assessment of these will be paramount. The asking price is generally not a mystery, of course, but once you understand the Cost of Renovation and the True Market Value, your decision to buy or not buy will become quite clear. Being able to determine the first two quickly will also help you overcome competition in competitive markets. You need to take as much time and do as much research as necessary to determine market value and renovation cost. Get comfortable in these two areas, because inaccuracy will lead to possible financial obstacles.

In addition to being vitally important to your deal, the investor hat will be the first one you put on in your quest to buy profitable real estate. As a savvy real estate investor, as you are in the marketplace making offers and looking at deals, one thing to understand is the importance of seeing results through consistency and follow-through. Stay on task and don't get distracted or discouraged. And don't let naysayers and negative people dissuade you. Listen only to those who have gotten to where you want to be in life.

In this book, I will mostly be discussing how to invest in *residential* real estate. My main experience and concentration are in the following areas:

1. Single-family Homes
2. Multi-family Units (up to four units)
3. Townhomes

There are plenty of good buys out there, no matter the market. If your offers are getting accepted too often, you are offering too much. To find the best deals, you'll want to build up "leads" for yourself—find all the avenues possible to locate investment real estate in your market, from which you can then select the best buys. Wherever your leads come from, whatever type of property you buy (which we'll examine shortly), you need to effect a certain dogged determination to follow up on what will often seem to be frustrating, dead-end leads. It is usually those types of leads that bring you properties that others have overlooked due to inexperience or laziness, and often those that will make you the most money.

It does not matter what the asking price is. You will make offers that make sense to you and your investments. You'll have no idea what the seller is thinking or what situation he or she is in, so don't assume how the seller will respond to your bid; make the offer and see what happens. I have made dozens of offers that I presumed the sellers would never go for, but they did. The "offers" part of real estate investment can be frustrating, and many people get discouraged and get out of the business because they never master the process. Don't let this pitfall get you. There are lots of deals at any given moment, and when you fully accept this, you will learn to block out negativity and the negative people who try to tell you what can't be done. Do you think Donald Trump gets rejections on his offers? Of course he does. Do you think he makes low-ball offers? Of course he does. Do you think he gets discouraged? Safe to say that he does not. What would have happened to his empire if he fell into this trap?

One of the first questions I am asked when I tell people what I do is: Where do I find my properties? I always answer, "There is no one way." If there were, if it were easy, you would just go to one source. But there are many ways to buy. Not surprisingly, leads and the property acquisitions that follow come from many different sources, but I have been the one with that "dogged determination," patience, and swift action that got me the deal at the best price. Here are some great sources for developing your sellers list:

- **Estates/Probate:** Someone's estate is the total of everything he or she owns. Probate is the process of legally establishing the validity of a will before a judicial authority. So, in the event of the death of a real estate owner without a will, sometimes courts must review and determine who now owns that property, and often some of this property needs to be sold. This process is done as a matter of public record, so you may look up probate notices in the legal notices section of your newspaper, determine if real estate properties are involved, and then make purchase offers as you see fit.
- **Tax Deeds:** When property taxes remain unpaid for a number of years (depending upon state and local laws), the appropriate county may eventually seize the property from the owner and sell it in what is commonly called a tax deed sale, as a way to recoup those delinquent property taxes. The opportunity for a real estate investor lies in the chance to get a property for much less than market value: for example, you may spend $10,000 on a plot of land that is worth $50,000. Keep in mind that this is a complicated process that requires a savvy investor with cash who is willing to do comprehensive research.
- **Real estate investors who wholesale their properties:** whether

owned or under contract by them.

These all represent what I call "wells," or sources of leads that I can go to and draw upon. When one "well" seems dry (though it will only be a temporary depletion), I go to others. Then back again, as needed. Remember: Be determined and patient, and stick to those leads that seem tough to get your hands on—the payoff can be well worth the work!

I develop potential inventory to purchase (my leads) from the above sources, and I analyze the investment potential of each. One thing I passionately believe is that time is our most vital asset. Therefore, I will teach you how be as efficient as possible because, yes, time <u>is</u> money. Keep in mind that most people reading this book have full-time jobs, so time is already not a luxury. Working smart and using the skills of others to assist you are important.

- **Networking:** This means getting out of your house and meeting people. Join local real estate clubs, volunteer at a local charity, whatever and wherever you can. Leads about properties for sale come from just about anywhere, and the more people who know you're a serious real estate investor, the more possibilities will come your way—many, seemingly from nowhere!

- **Realtors:** You will want to work with more than one Realtor if possible. They are in the trenches day in and day out, and most have a feel for current trends in sales and prices. They work on a strictly commission basis. They get paid only if they bring you a deal, and even then they get paid by the seller. You need to find Realtors who are on the same page as you. If you are looking for investment properties, work with Realtors who know how to find these specific types of properties. If the Realtor you are working with is not motivated or organized, or has no understanding of what you want, move on to the next. You want to work with agents who are motivated, organized, and efficient. Remember that this is your business, and you want to work with serious people who are not going to waste your time. You must work with Realtors who understand the investment part of this business, or are willing to adjust their business to your criteria. What do I mean? Well, there are lots of Realtors out there, and you need to find the right one. If you are working with someone who does not understand the investment side and is not willing to adjust to your way of thinking, you must move on to the next agent. For example, have you ever walked into a clothing store and asked the salesperson for a pair of pants, and he takes you to the shirts section? How do you feel at that moment? Frustrated, and clearly the salesperson is not on the same page or not a good listener. Once you find a good Realtor, treat him or her well, and the Realtor will make you a lot of money. Realtors have access to the MLS service, which has most of the current market offerings listed. The MLS is available via computer with up-to-date info on listings, prices, and much more. Work only with Realtors who use email and the Internet to transfer information to you. You don't want Realtors who fax their leads. It will take up a lot of paper and toner, and it will not be as clear as email. Only work through email; it's much more efficient and clearer and much easier to track. Remember: You, as an investor, represent repeat business to a Realtor. How many houses does a homeowner buy in his or her lifetime? Three, perhaps. You, on the other hand, are looking to buy all the time. Think about that; the Realtors should go the extra mile for you. So, they are usually more than happy to spend some time learning about you and your aspirations in real estate.

- **Banks:** Inquire at as many banks as you can about foreclosure properties that they own. Bankers must foreclose on properties where the loans have gone seriously into default. The properties become part of the bank's Real Estate Owned (REO) portfolios, which are listed in their books as nonperforming loans. Banks are in the money business for the most part, not the real estate business, and they sell these properties to private real estate investors like you.

Pre-foreclosures: Unfortunately, for many reasons, people

sometimes fall far behind on their mortgages. It is usually better for them to sell before the bank forecloses on the property, which will damage their credit further and cause additional grief to all concerned. Sometimes, you as an investor can help out these folks and find great properties for your portfolio. I often run ads offering to buy homes so owners may avoid foreclosure. Try your local free newspapers to get started. You are looking to attract homeowners who are behind on their mortgages and looking to sell their homes to pay off the mortgage and late fees. The ad should read like this: "Behind on your mortgage? Let me help you."

For Sale By Owners (FSBOs): Many homeowners prefer to sell their homes on their own, rather than engage a real estate salesperson. There are many reasons why they do so, some good, some bad, but this can be a rich source of leads for you. Track down as many as you can by driving through neighborhoods, on the lookout for "For Sale" signs, and by studying the classified ads. Do your homework, and then offer a price that you are certain would be a bargain for you. If they take it, great. If they don't, move on. Either way, you will eventually end up with some fine properties by pursuing private sellers. Remember, if a lot of your offers are accepted, that means your offers are too high. Sometimes sellers are offended by my low offers. What I like to tell sellers who are insulted by my offer is basically: "If you are insulted by my offer, I am insulted by your asking price." Either way, keep your emotion out of it.

A note about sellers: I think it's important to realize why people sell properties, if for nothing else than to be able to gauge how motivated they are to sell.

Perhaps they are investors themselves and want to take a profit (or cut a loss), and this is their "exit strategy." For many sellers, they are moving out of the area due to a new job in a new town. (If this were you, how anxious would you be to sell?) Sometimes, investors buy a home to fix and sell and perhaps run out of money and now need to get out. I have purchased properties form other investors who either ran out of money or made mistakes and just wanted out. Many of these were already rehabbed.

Properties that are distressed and in need of renovation are the most common. Once a property is not in market condition, it's very hard to attain a conventional loan to buy that property. Therefore, cash or private money may be the only way to sell that property. This, in most cases, will only allow investors to purchase and, hence, give someone like you an opportunity. Others, as we'll later see, have run into financial roadblocks that might spell trouble if they don't sell soon.

See what I mean? The reasons behind the sale, as well as the motivation of the seller, can be another telling piece of the large puzzle you are solving. Once you understand how to analyze an investment, the rest is just going through the motions. A lot of things in life work as a numbers game. You want to throw as much mud on the wall as you can to see what will stick and what won't. But the more mud you throw, the better chances you have of mud sticking. (Why you would want mud on your walls is another question altogether . . .)

The Appraiser Hat

As an investor, you need to take advantage of your market's tax roll, or tax records. "Tax records" is one industry term for property information gathered by counties. It is public information and accessible by anyone. This information can often be comprehensive and is one of the best tools for analyzing the appropriateness of real estate investments.

The Internet is a great way to access property tax information. You can also use the services of companies that offer tax roll information and "comps" (the value of comparable properties) for a fee, either per search or monthly. You might choose to start, if your checkbook allows, with a professional search service; then, study their process and results and use that information to leverage your own knowledge and flatten your learning curve so that you can do it on your own later. Another way for a new investor to get a feel for market value is to work with plenty of Realtors. They can provide you with detailed information. Just make sure to give them your business whenever you can.

Determining the correct True Market Value presents one of the greatest pitfalls in real estate investing. If you buy a $90,000 property for $100,000, you're starting out $10,000 in the hole—not necessarily fatal, but given a choice, not the best option, either. Similarly, when you are selling a property, you will nearly always be selling to a buyer who must obtain financing to do the deal. The price you are selling for means little if the appraised value comes up short; banks will lend on the contract price or the appraisal price, whichever is *less*. If the buyer's appraiser comes in $10,000 under the selling price, the buyer must come up with another $10,000 to close, but more likely, he or she will just walk away, now convinced that the property is a poor investment.

Establishing yourself with local appraisers is very important. They know the market better than most—it's their job. Finding someone dependable who you can get to know and build a personal relationship with can be the difference between getting the best deals and missing out. If you are working with a Realtor, and you want a second opinion on the market value, you can request what is called a "pencil search" from a licensed appraiser. This is an unofficial valuation report, but often a good indicator of how the written report will come in. The appraiser often won't charge you, but if he or she does, it will usually be very reasonable and certainly worth it. So make it a point to go out on a regular basis and meet and greet with competent appraisers near you. They will be glad to get to know someone who may be a fine source of future business. It's a classic win/win situation.

While you will have no reason to become a licensed appraiser yourself, you'll still want to learn as much as you can about the appraisal process. The market constantly changes. Appraising is an art, not a science. Once you have all the information you can possibly gather, trust your instincts *without being blinded by the excitement of closing the deal.* Pushing a less-than-promising deal through, whatever the risks, is one of the most common mistakes made by new investors. Remember, there are always other deals coming down the road. Yes, you will miss a few good buys, but it is better to miss some and wait for the next one than to buy something that turns into a costly mistake.

As you begin to look at neighborhoods, ask yourself: How much are rents in the area? Are homes selling quickly? (You can determine this by how often homes actually sell and how many days they were on the market. Get this info from your local real estate agent.) Does the area appear to be growing? (Learn if there has been a lot of construction activity in the area.) How old is the neighborhood? (Look at the tax roll for the era most of the homes were built, which you can get from local Realtors.) What kinds of price ranges are available on the market and what is the cost per square foot of homes? Are the homes nearby well maintained and clean, and are the lawns kept up? Is there shopping nearby, and are there churches and schools within a short driving distance?

When doing your research for market value, look for similar

properties that were sold within the last three to six months, because the market is ever-changing, and you want only the most recent trends. In the same vein, keep your geographic search in as narrow a market area as possible. Expand only when necessary to find similar "comps." You want to compare "apple-to-apple" comps of similar square footage, construction, number of bedrooms and bathrooms, lot size, date of construction, and neighborhood characteristics, combining all the tax information with the physical research as you progress.

I realize all this can seem a bit daunting to a newbie, but I promise, you will find yourself familiar with these terms a whole lot quicker than you may imagine as you progress through this book. In the beginning of my real-estate career, I used my Realtor to give me the market values and closed sales. Whenever I needed more assurance, I backed up the Realtor's estimate with a report from a licensed appraiser. You must get the market value right because everything else works off the market value. A single, well-written appraisal, studied for a few weeks, will provide you with a solid background of knowledge. Do your research and homework, and learn what you know and what you don't know. (Knowing what you don't know is important; you should start researching and strengthening the areas that you are weak in.) Get to know local appraisers. Take them out to lunch and pick their brains. You'll be amazed at how much you can learn by just having a friendly conversation.

Start with this overview of the appraiser's process:

There are three primary approaches to appraising: The *Sales Comparison Approach*, the *Cost Approach*, and the *Income Approach.*

The basic approach to Sales Comparison appraising is the following:

Determine the price of comparable properties by analyzing properties sold in the same area, of similar size, and within the last three to six months.

You may also check out the Cost Approach, which means you determine the cost of building a new home like the one you're considering buying, then subtract the price of improvements to the property that would make it as new, and finally add the value of the lot on which the property stands.

Finally, you may want to examine the Income Approach to the property in question. Here, you look at the net operating income of a property (income after expenses). If you are looking to purchase properties for rental, basically analyzing the cash flow will determine what someone is willing to invest, as well as market value.

When you do seek a professional appraisal, the appraiser will use the following list to determine the price:

1. List data needed to do the job and list sources
2. Gather, record, and verify all information
3. Determine the best use of the property
4. Estimate the land value
5. Estimate property value by each of the three approaches
6. Reconcile the estimated values and produce a final estimate of value

I cannot stress enough the importance of understanding how to determine market value! Since appraising is an art, not a science, this is a complicated topic. Becoming a real estate appraiser is a most complex and lengthy process. As a real estate investor, you're not required to go out and get an appraiser license, but you do need to learn as much as you can; not necessarily to do an appraiser's job but rather to learn all the important aspects of how an appraiser comes up with a value. Paying too much is simply paying too much—it can't be rescued with some magic formula that allows you to find hidden value when such value doesn't exist. An old real estate pro once said, "I make my money when I *buy* the property." Get it?

The Contractor Hat

One of the best ways to find real estate deals is to look for properties that need some work—from a modest amount of fixing up to a complete renovation. You'll need to figure out the cost and then determine who will do the necessary work. Must you do some of the work yourself? Personally, I have purchased and sold hundreds of properties but have never picked up a hammer in my life. If I need a light bulb changed, I call an electrician. (I am not the most mechanical or handiest guy in the industry. My wife is the handy one in my home. For her last birthday, I bought her a drill set; it was funny at first, but then she frowned at me and said, "Now where are the diamonds?")

If you are handy, that's fine, and it can't hurt a bit. But if you aren't, no need to worry. Either way, you'll want to decide at some point how much time you want to devote to being a real estate investor and how much time to being a contractor (that is, decide when it is to your economic advantage to change hats). Remembering that time is your most important asset, you need to get a feel for what is the best (most profitable) task for you to be involved with at any given moment.

No matter how much work you decide to do yourself, there is something you'll want to do at every stage of the learning process: *Study.* Some textbook stuff, yes, but mostly a lot of good old-fashioned, on-the-job training. For instance, an easy way to learn about the basic costs of materials is to spend time haunting your local hardware store, Home Depot, Lowes, or other building supply center. Bring along a legal pad. Study and jot down the prices of bathroom fixtures, carpeting, and kitchens. You'll end up with a feel for prices, and you'll learn the lingo of home improvement and renovation. More arrows in your quiver.

Go to the library and grab a handbook on home improvement.

Again, you'll not only learn the basics of home repairs, but you'll also become familiar with common terms. Even if you hire someone to do the work (perhaps especially if you do), you're going to want to understand the standard terminology and the buzzwords that your contractor throws at you. If not, what she says may sound something like, "Yep, the hugegotter is no good, and we have to gold leaf the rim of the forleshem." You *could* just grin and nod, worried that you are going to give away that you're new at this, but you may end up grinning and nodding your way to a huge bill for repairs and upgrades you never wanted. Learn the lingo and learn the prices. You'll be surprised by how much you can digest in just a few weeks.

Speaking of contractors, build a solid Rolodex of leads here, too. Reasonably-priced contractors who are competent and dependable and understand investors are in notoriously short supply. Use the networking skills we discussed earlier for finding renovation contacts. When you try a new contractor, start with a small job; test him for quality and honesty before handing over big jobs. Get it all in writing and be very careful! But once you do find the right contractors, treat 'em like gold—because the good ones are as good as gold in your pocket. At the same time, you don't want to under-spend, either. Only wealthy people can afford "cheap" because they will have to do it over and over again. Remember that.

Another decision that comes with each deal is: How much renovation do you need to do? Sounds obvious, but you want to go into this with a conscious consideration of the issues, and, as the flip side of going on the cheap, you want to *be very wary of overdoing your upgrades.* Most new investors don't skip things that need doing; most over-renovate! They get emotionally involved (which is always a danger at any stage of investing) and spend money as though they were going to live in the property themselves. Resist this urge and remember: Every dollar you spend in renovation is a dollar less profit you'll realize. Don't cut necessary corners, don't do anything to less than "code" (adhering to necessary building and safety codes), but don't buy fancy fixtures just because you think the color matches your eyes. Spend wisely on things that will increase the value and salability of the property.

All of this "contractor hat" knowledge will be vital, not only when you need to actually do renovations or repairs, but even before you buy a property. Until you get good at estimating renovation costs on your own, use contractor bids to estimate your costs. With every estimate that you get from a contractor on homes you are looking to purchase, your knowledge base should increase.

Put your new knowledge to use with one of the first decision processes the investor must use: What is your "exit strategy?" Are you going to rent it long-term? Fix it up and "flip" it? Something in between? When you are analyzing a new property, mull over the process that began with your analysis of the best use of the property and the best approach to renovation; you should have an accurate cost of repairs (which will depend on your personal goals), one that will take you to the next level in your investment decision.

When I look at a piece of real estate for potential purchase, I first ask myself: "What is my exit strategy?" This will make a difference in how I analyze my renovation expense. For example, if I identify the property as a rental, I will not put in fancy kitchens or expensive bathroom fixtures, because the tenants will not, for the most part, treat it like their own. On the flip side, if I want to resell, I will renovate the property to the level of my competitors who are selling in the area.

The way I analyze properties is as follows: I always have a licensed contractor confirm my initial estimate of renovation during the inspection period of my contract (during this period I can bail out, but once I am under contract it's my problem). In other words, if I thought a renovation was going to cost me $10,000 and my contractor comes back and tells me it will cost $15,000, I simply exercise my "subject to" clause or renegotiate my offer.

Let's do a sample property walk-through, and I'll share my thought processes as I determine the condition of the property and what it should cost to renovate it.

First, I count beds and baths (it may not always be accurate from other sources such as the tax roll). I jot this and all other info down on a legal pad. Then, I measure each room for square footage.

Next, I examine the windows to see if any need to be repaired or replaced. I look at the framing to determine if it's obviously broken or damaged, and I operate each window to determine how well it works.

Then it's on to the floors, whether made of wood or tile, or carpeted. Are any of these worn-out looking, broken, or missing?

What about walls? I look for dirt, holes in the wallboard, or whether any kind of repair is required before painting.

Then, to the bathrooms. I look at the wall tiles and judge their condition. The tub is next. Is it beat-up and in need of replacement, or can it simply be resurfaced? Does the toilet need to be replaced? I also check out the vanity (the cabinet in which the sink is placed).

In the kitchen, I want to determine if it requires complete replacement or if I can save money by refurbishing it instead.

The electrical system is vital, of course. I check out the fuse box—does it look old and broken?

I check the ceiling for signs of leakage, which can indicate that the roof has serious issues.

I count how many doors, exterior and interior, need replacing. I check out the baseboards and molding for their condition. Then I go outside the house.

I want to determine if I need some basic landscaping improvements such as new fencing, sod or grass, or any other "curb appeal" issues.

All of this tells me what the house needs to come back to market condition. Do try to be thoughtful and thorough when it is your turn.

When I walk out of that home after my initial inspection, I want to come out with the approximate dollar amount for the combined material and labor that would be required to bring the property back to market condition. As previously discussed, determining the wrong market value could hurt your investment. The same holds for renovation costs. Be conservative and take your time when analyzing the renovation expense. Until you develop solid relationships with those who will do the work for you (contractors, handymen), have enough sense not to pull the trigger on something unknown.

I also calculate a percentage for unforeseen expenses that I add to the renovation. For example, if the renovation is $10,000, I will add 5% as unforeseen expense to make my renovation $10,500. By all means, if you're not sure or if you see something beyond your scope of knowledge, take your time and seek a professional quote.

For more information on all the topics covered in this section, visit my website at www.TheRoadToRealEstateWealth.com.

The Lawyer Hat

At this point, you may have found a suitable potential real estate investment, or you may be ready to make an offer. You've looked over the property and the public information available about it, but you're not ready to buy it just yet.

Time to cross your t's and dot your i's. You have a contract to deal with. Think about that word: contract. The definition for our purpose is, "A legally binding agreement between two or more parties."

The contract, to me, is the cash register tape. It records many details of the transaction and whatever is written there really does matter, especially should any (shall we say) complications arise during the whole process, from purchase all the way through your disposal of the property. Here is where many people falter. But don't despair. This is where *you* can work smarter than the next guy or gal. This is where you can use the dreaded minutiae to your decided advantage! Let me explain.

There are many different kinds of contracts out there. Some we call "standard contracts," in that they have been drawn up by unbiased lawyers to be as fair as possible to both sides of the transaction. This type of contract will deal with the customary practices of any particular state. Though negotiable, the language in the contract will stay unbiased to either party in the contract. Samples of these are published and sold through local realty boards or even through office supply and business superstores. I suggest you buy one of these samples and become thoroughly familiar with it, then use a highlighter pen, and make certain you understand every detail. As an investor, you must understand what the customary responsibilities are for each party to that contract. This contract is not typically used when dealing with experienced sellers (i.e., other investors and banks and the like). But if such a standard contract is used in the investor market, an addendum may be attached that can tilt certain terms in favor of one party or another. Once you understand the terms of the basic contract, you will better understand when a seller is attempting to tip the scales in his favor. Also, in a competitive market and when time is of the essence, some investors take too long to refer a contract to their lawyer; this is usually because the investor does not sufficiently understand contracts and is afraid of making an error. If you, on the other hand, profoundly understand your contract terms, you may not always have to have every detail checked out by an attorney, and you can probably move faster than some of the other guys.

As a new investor, you should take as much time as you need to get comfortable with and informed about contracts. Don't ever sign something you don't understand, even if it means passing on a deal. Many investors sign contracts without reading and understanding all the details of the contract. What you agree to by signing the contract is what you will have to abide by.

There are also "seller-biased contracts." Just like they sound, the seller's attorney has drawn them up so as to stack as much as possible in the seller's favor. I want you to understand what to look for in such contracts, how to help make sure that you don't get hurt, and how to stack the odds in *your* favor. The contract itself can end up making you (or saving you, which is the same thing) thousands of dollars if you approach it correctly.

As you enter this business, what other books may not tell you, or at least they give short shrift to, is that you will often run up against other investors competing for the same properties (or selling properties you may want), and many of these other investors are smart and experienced. You need to be prepared to counter the many terms and conditions in the contract that are favorable to them. Because, as a new buyer, you will be making offers to sellers who are armed with biased contracts, you may run into a plethora of details that can damage you. For example, the deposits may be higher than usual, the closing dates shorter, the inspections tighter and with less "outs" in the form of buyer contingencies. All of these will push you, as a buyer, to take action more quickly than you may want to. Having a clear understanding of these engineered pitfalls will allow you to move fast but still minimize the risk of damage. Remember: Anything can be written into a contract, from the patently fair to the profoundly ridiculous, so you need to be meticulous, read every word, and understand every concept and clause. And you need to be able to do this as quickly as possible because time is of the essence. Once you sign, those concepts and details must be adhered to; your choices have been made.

If you don't abide by the agreement, you are in default. You could lose your deposit, the property, and, worse, potentially end up involved in a lawsuit.

One thing I ask you never to forget during the contract proceedings: *Everything is negotiable.* Don't be shy. Ask for things. You've probably heard the word "no" a few times in your life! So don't be overly sensitive. In fact, developing tougher skin will help you in all of your real estate endeavors. Another thing: do more work and be more detail-oriented than the competition. Now you know that most people don't read their real estate contracts. Since you will read *yours* with great care and "massage" it to favor your side as much as possible, you can gain a real leg up.

Here's an example. When I'm selling, my contracts state that the buyer will pay all closing costs. Customarily, the seller pays *some* of the closing costs, but this is not the law or a moral obligation or anything of the sort—it is simply a part of the negotiation process. Often, at a late point in the closing, a buyer will notice this clause in the contract and ask me about it. I simply point to the contract and tell him that "It's all right there." He has to decide if he wants the property under the current contract, and if he pushes, I can decide if I am willing to pay the selling costs or walk away instead. Again, contracts are negotiating tools and should be used to get as much as you can out of the deal. This is business! A small amount of money here or there can make or break any investment, and it is vital that you gain every advantage you can. Especially here, in this arena of creative real estate investing (that is, you're not simply buying a home that you will live in for the next 20 years). You are entering an unconventional part of real estate; there is no reason for the contracts to be conventional.

So, what do most people read? Only the front page, I'm afraid—the address, price, and closing date. *You* must read every word. Yes, much of it is lawyerly gibberish that is hardly as enthralling as *Gone with the Wind.* But now you know how vital every word is. Don't let all those Wherefores and Hereins confound you. Be sure to familiarize yourself with the terminology and topics. Highlight everything you don't fully understand and then look it all up or, further, get someone to explain every nuance to you.

Here are some important things to look for as you examine the contract:

1. Make certain you have the right address and folio number (the ID of the property according to the tax roll).

2. Check the price and deposit amount and who is holding the deposit. It's always best to give the money to a Title Insurance Company (more on these later) than to give the money directly to the seller—you never know what can happen, and you would be very upset if a seller disappeared with your deposit money!

3. Check the dateline of the Closing Date.

4. Check the Closing Costs and make certain they are no more than customary if you are paying those costs.

5. Check the Evidence of Title; this is your proof that the owner is really who you think it is and that there are no undisclosed liens on the property for loans against it or unpaid contactor's bills or the like. I've had titles on properties I was about to buy come up as not "clean." What does that mean? Understand that *actual* ownership is a legal definition. Just because you live in a property and the mortgage is in your name doesn't mean you have complete legal ownership, nor does it mean that you can pass ownership to someone else. Ownership of a property is a matter of public record; you must "record" your deed with the county where the property is located. This process ensures that the ownership of all properties is a part of the public record. Anyone at any given time can access these public records and see who owns the subject property. With real estate ownership, you're letting the whole world know what properties you own. (All of this work is done by a title company, so don't worry about having to do it yourself. Anyway, the title company works for free until the day of the closing.)

Similarly, mortgages are a part of the public record. Any lender or lending institution needs be certain that the buyer of a property on which she holds a mortgage knows that the mortgage must be paid off before the seller can transfer ownership.

Another issue: Every city has certain requirements that property owners must adhere to. When owners don't comply, the city uses techniques similar to what a mortgage holder may use by recording a lien against the property. There also may be monetary fines involved for non-compliance. For instance, each city has building codes. These codes exist to ensure minimum housing standards and to guarantee that property taxes are collected on all real estate within the city's jurisdiction. So cities may place a lien or violation on a property for a variety of reasons: taxes due, utilities unpaid, an owner having work done without a permit, and more. Fines may also be involved. These city actions form another "cloud" on the property title and may prevent the legal sale of the property. Sometimes, the seller may not be aware of the extent of the title issue, or even that any issue exists.

So how do all these issues of title affect you as a potential buyer? You need to be able to buy properties that don't have any of these issues clouding legal ownership. As a buyer, you will not always have control of these, but you can work with the seller to "cure" any issues that arise. Many closings get postponed or delayed because the owner cannot yet transfer legal ownership to you if these issues are not cleared up. It doesn't matter that you're ready to buy; if the seller can't properly transfer ownership to you because of issues of title, you may have to wait or even walk away, depending upon the issue or the willingness of the seller to cooperate.

Remember: When you sign the contract to purchase the property, make sure you understand the title section of the contract. For example, if you sign a contract that states you are buying the property with a title defect (which is not the norm), then you will not have the option to walk away without losing your deposit.

Typically, you must make certain the contract states that the *title be free, clear, and marketable before* closing and that the seller cannot force you to buy a property that has title defects.

Don't worry about having to do all the research. This is where title companies come in. These firms search the public records to track the chain of ownership for the property to ensure that the current owner is providing legal title without any liens or violations; this can include making certain that all obligations of the owner and the property itself are current, including the payment of taxes, liens, and utilities.

Once these searches are done and shown to be clear, the title company, just like any other insurance company, will provide a commitment letter and insurance policy. This is "title insurance," which protects the buyer against loss due to an oversight on the title company's part (most lenders require title insurance). Some examples include the following: A previous lender has an outstanding note or mortgage on your property before you owned it, and is now making claim against you for payment of that note. Or, you are about to sell a property, and a new title company does its search only to find that the deed you received was in fact flawed, because one person who had partial legal ownership never signed off on the sale. Since you don't have complete legal ownership of the property, you can't sell it! But, as you received title insurance when you bought the property, the title insurance company must make certain you don't sustain a loss on your original investment.

6. Be certain to be on the look-out for any "Addendum" or additions to the standard contract format. These usually are in the other party's favor, and you don't want to be responsible for fulfilling certain conditions as laid out in the Addendum that will cost you later, or agree to something unfavorable hidden in the Addendum that will not allow you to walk away from the deal or even cause you to lose your deposit.

It bears repeating: the contract *you sign* is what counts! If you run into trouble, you will have to adhere to the signed agreement—good reason to understand exactly what you are signing. If you don't feel comfortable dealing with all these details at this point, bring in an attorney. (It can get terribly expensive hiring a lawyer just for contract work, but be safe until you are ready to go it on your own.)

Another option is to work with a title company that will send a representative along with you to the closing, if this is common practice in your state. Title companies have staff attorneys who may assist with closing. Eventually, along with your own diligent study and work, this

may be all you need. Title companies make money from the closing, so they have a vested interest that can give you a bit more leverage.
One excellent tool you should use is called the "contingency clause." Others use the more vitriolic name "weasel clause." This contract technique allows you to place contingencies into the agreement whereby you may be able to back out of the deal with your deposit intact, if necessary, when something does not go as you'd like. In other words, if for some reason you don't wish to, or you're not able to, complete a deal, these contingencies will give you a legal basis for stepping away without losing your deposit or being subject to a lawsuit. Such typical contingencies may be as follows:

- Your ability to secure financing: Since financing is the biggest hurdle for an investor, you could otherwise lose your deposit if you cannot secure the type and amount of financing that you need.
- Your right to inspect the property: Here, you can make certain that the real estate matches your original renovation estimates.
- Your ability to sell another property that is on the market: Occasionally, a buyer needs to sell one property in order to move some funds from that sale into the current purchase. This clause often prevents the buyer from financially over-extending himself or herself.
- Subject to free and clear title: This ensures that the buyer will receive a clear title, free of any encumbrances.
- Wholesale the property: If you put the property under contract to purchase and don't intend to actually close on the deal (instead, you plan to assign or "wholesale" your deal), but you don't find a buyer in time, then you can exercise your weasel clause.

You can amplify some of these with a little creative wording. For instance, in the first example above, part of the financial provisions gives the buyer time to obtain "suitable financing." Here, use your new knowledge of financing to your advantage. If the lowest prevailing interest rate you know you can obtain is 6%, write in that you will need a rate of 5.5%. You won't get that rate, and you know it, but this will give you an out. Remember, this is business, which means using your unbeatable work ethic and growing knowledge of buying techniques to give yourself every possible advantage.

Theoretically at least, you can use any reason (some would say any excuse), but of course, most sellers won't let you tie up their property and effectively take it off the market and then back out for the weakest of reasons. But as a rule of thumb, even experienced sellers and banks will give you an inspection period in which you can confirm your assessments.

One more tip: At times, consider what some call the "Red Herring" technique. Here, you ask for something in the contract that you don't really want or care about. It could be furniture currently in the home, for example. You write in the contract that all furniture on site will remain and become your property upon closing. Of course, at the same time, you may write an offer for less than their asking price, but you want them to focus on the furniture question instead. This technique doesn't work every time (what does?), but it will work often enough to become an important part of your investor toolbox. I recommend that you read each contract from start to finish and highlight everything you don't understand, then do your research.

The Salesperson Hat

Now let's talk about a skill that should be part of every businessperson's arsenal: SELLING. Whether you are a shoe salesperson, president of the United States, or anything in-between, you will find that much of your success centers on your ability to listen, to be persuasive, and to help others make decisions. Here, we'll look at selling, marketing, and even see how our overall strategy should influence how we market and sell.

One excellent sales process is based upon the AIDA model:

1. Attention: get the customer's attention
2. Interest: stimulate the customer's interest
3. Desire: create desire to buy
4. Action: confirm the action the buyer must show you to get the deal done

Question Right to Get the Sale

The idea is to discover the real objectives here. Remember, you will not sell the property itself so much as *sell the benefits* that the buyer will receive. For instance, the buyer will learn that he or she can, by owning a property, save thousands of dollars in income taxes every year. One of the most important techniques for getting all this done is to know your product! You can in turn use this knowledge to educate your buyers, to help them find what's best for them.

Marketing is another area where most investors skimp on *learning and follow-through,* so you can be a giant step ahead of them by learning more and working harder than they are willing to! Remember, if you don't sell the property, you aren't going to realize any profit. When, if you sell it, you'll naturally want to realize the highest possible price. That is done through the best possible sales and marketing. More, you need to become a *promoter.*

You know what? Most investors don't start to market their property until they are ready to sell it. I start promoting, selling, and marketing as soon as I put the property under contract. If you have a property under contract for, say, 30 days, no one but you has the right to buy that property. This means you have 30 days to get a head start on earning a profit from it, without incurring any mortgage costs or other major expenses during that time. Might as well get a jump on things! Use your growing network of contacts to generate early interest in your deal. Get started thinking about the best uses of Realtors, email, direct mail postcards, newspaper classified ads, flyers, and everything else that you will eventually use to market your property (we'll get into this in much more detail later.) And keep in mind: When selling a product, you need as many leads as possible, and you need to keep them coming! I remember a friend of mine decided to sell his car. He placed an ad in the newspaper and quickly had four or five people interested (or, for our purposes, four or five leads). He cancelled the ad, thinking the car was as good as sold. Nope. Not one potential buyer even called back, much less showed up, despite their professed keen interest. My buddy ended up with no leads and had to start the ad all over again with the loss of weeks of time. It can take dozens, even hundreds of leads to close a deal. You'll want to ensure that you have so many leads on hand that *someone* will buy.

What about the actual selling? Perhaps you've never had a sales job (though as we mentioned, nearly every job involves some selling; you sold *yourself* to get the job in the first place). First, listen more than talk. Does this surprise you? You may think selling is talking non-stop, overpowering people's objections and wearing them down—not in this business. Some of the old-time sales pros did it this way. As times changed, so did selling. Now, it is generally agreed that *consultative selling* is the superior approach. My grandmother used to tell me that God gave me two ears but only one mouth, and that there was a good reason. So let's say you listen twice as much as you speak. For every statement you foist on your customer, ask two questions.

Remember you are selling real estate, and this often will be the largest purchase your clients make during their lifetimes. It's not like a pair of shoes or a TV set, where the buyer is in and out of the store in half an hour and that's the end of it.

Here are some questions I usually ask of customers:

- Where do you live now? (I learn what kind of neighborhood they are used to.)
- Do you rent or do you own? (If they have already qualified for a home loan, the odds that they can qualify for my property are better than for the average renter.)
- Are they looking to live in the property or use it as an investment? (Their goals will help determine if any particular property is right for them.)

There is only so much a person can do with a piece of real estate. A person is buying it to live in, buying it to sell it, or buying it to rent for income cash flow.

If the person is looking to buy the home to live in, there are questions I ask that help me qualify the buyer. During my first conversation, I can find out a lot about my future buyer. At the same time, I want to work only with those who will "do what I ask them to do." For example, if I asked the buyer to go ahead and check out the property and call me back and he or she does so, that's a good indication that the person is not interested in wasting my time. At the same time, if I ask the buyer to talk to a mortgage broker for future pre-qualifications, and he does that, I have another good indication that the buyer is serious.

As you start developing your buyers list, you need to be able to properly organize yourself by tracking who you talk to, when you talk to them, and what was discussed. As a seller, I need to be able to properly follow up so I don't waste my time.

When I'm trying to sell the property to an investor, I need to ask different kind of questions, such as the following:

- Have you bought in the past? (I'm trying to determine his experience level.)

If he has bought something in the past, I ask questions about the previous transactions. How did you pay for the property? (If the investor is trying to buy a handyman property that would be hard to mortgage, I may need to educate the buyer on different ways of financing properties that are not in market condition.)

What kinds of properties are you interested in? (Single-family home, multifamily homes, condos, townhomes)

Are you interested in anything that makes sense as an investment; in other words, in anything that makes you money?

I have three categories that I place potential investment buyers in. I try to categorize their knowledge and experience level to get a feel for whom I'm talking to.

The first category is new investors. New investors are investors who have never purchased an investment property before. These investors need a heavy amount of educating and selling, all at the same time. You see, new investors are frightened because of their lack of knowledge and uncertainty. Therefore, I try to hold their hands throughout the transaction.

The next category is investors who have done a few deals but still have a bit to learn. These investors require some support but are somewhat experienced.

At the next level are the experienced investors. You don't need to coach them. They usually know what they're doing.

Even the greatest sales approach won't ensure that you get every deal. Nor should it. Part of the beauty of the consultative approach is that people find out what they need and want. As we progress in the book, I will show you, by using cases studies, the different techniques that I used to sell my properties.

Some people have a great deal of cash, but not many. Few investors are sitting on hundreds of thousands of dollars. It isn't Monopoly money that is used for real estate deals! This is why explaining how mortgages work is another aspect of real estate sales. Very few people buy with all cash, so their ability to understand and find financing is vital, as is your ability to ask questions and work only with buyers who will most likely be able to secure financing. I personally started with nothing—even worse, my work was irregular at the time, and I was still paying off college debts. So don't despair if you are in the same boat or worse. The key is finding the right deal and having the knowledge to make it work; the money will flow to these deals. And your enhanced selling skills will only make the money flow faster.

A final note about selling. Remember, even before you bid on the property you should have some idea of your end game, or "exit strategy" and how you plan to buy the property, use it, and sell it. You might rent the property and sell it later, or quickly retail it to a prospective homeowner who will want to live there, or find another real estate investor to purchase it. All of these are legitimate, but each approach has a different plan for sale—and yes, even before that, for purchase.

The Financing Hat

In much of the world, the use of creative financing can be rare. I feel certain that if I had stayed abroad, I probably would not have had the same opportunities that America has given me. Here in America, creative financing is part and parcel of most real estate transactions. "Leverage," in the financial sense, that is, creatively using a small amount of money to control investments worth considerably more, is vital to most deals. Knowledge of money markets, financing, mortgages, and qualifying for loans will be as important to your success in real estate as your knowledge of real estate itself.

First you need to understand that there are several different types of financing: Conventional, Hard Money, and Private Money.

"Conventional" or regular, long-term financing.

How do you attain these types of loans? From mortgage brokers and banks. The mortgage broker or mortgage banker may be your most important ally when selling properties. What is a mortgage broker? Someone who connects lenders with a financial institution that can provide a mortgage for a particular property. The broker draws from a pool of lenders to find the right match for each client.

What does a mortgage broker need to know in order to do her job? She must know how to read a credit score. She must know how to qualify someone for a loan, using income, cash on hand, and the analyzed credit score. She must understand what lenders look for to qualify the property itself: the appraisal, the condition of the real estate, the status, any special conditions the lender has, and more. Every broker must understand both the borrower's needs and requirements and the often subtle mechanics of each mortgage and its terms.

Some help will come from professionals we have already

discussed—lawyers, mortgage brokers, and bankers. Most of the time, each pro will make the most money when your deal actually goes through successfully. As you work with and get to know people in these fields, use them as information sources. Don't be shy about asking! You are a customer, and most pros realize that repeat customers are the best customers, and they should be willing to dedicate time to educating you and explaining the intricacies of the transaction. Sit down with each, keeping three goals in mind: 1) To get as much information and useful opinion as possible about the specific deal you are working on, 2) To learn as much as you can about financing and mortgages as possible, for your long-term education, and 3) To find ways to get the best possible financing—the best terms and rates—on this specific buy as possible. This third point is always vital. Every dollar saved will mean a dollar more of profit in the end. And by saving with every possible detail at every turn, this can translate into thousands of dollars more in total profits!

I personally have worked with more mortgage brokers than banks, and usually prefer the brokers. While banks sometimes have favorable rates, they prefer dealing with customers who fit into the little boxes they understand. Very often, if you and your situation cannot be crammed into that little box, you don't get the money, and you don't get your property. Mortgage brokers tend to work with many banks and sources of financing. Mortgage brokers will work to find the lender you fit with, not the other way around. They won't make any money if they don't close the deal, whereas most bankers are salaried, and if the deal doesn't go through, well, they still get paid, so why should they go out of their way for you? If you own your own home and perhaps have some equity in the home, getting a line of credit is a good way to raise some money to work with. I know many new and seasoned investors who get lines of credit secured by their personal residence. This works like a credit card where you only pay for what you use, and the rate is tied to whatever the current market is doing.

Mortgage brokers are more likely to custom-fit the financing arrangement to your needs. Ultimately, of course, you won't know how good a broker is until you've actually closed some deals. I often get solicited by mortgage brokers. Not all are created equal. You need a broker who speaks your language. In other words, you need a broker who is experienced in working with investors like you, someone who is not scared off by distressed deals and is self-motivated. Look for a good mesh of your personalities, as well. This is someone who becomes part of your extended sales force, after all. And, just like the appraisal process, you must understand everything about the process that can be gleaned without actually closing. The closing may take 30 to 45 days, and that is a lot of time to waste if the deal does not go through because you didn't do your homework.

Your understanding of credit and mortgages will not only serve you when you buy, but also when you are ready to sell and realize your profit. You don't want to waste time, as so many newcomers do, dealing with prospects who can never get financing. At the very least, a buyer will usually need credit, a job, and some money to put down. Here again, put your decorum and shyness aside, and ask questions of a potential buyer as soon as he or she shows interest in your property. This is a screening process and lets you focus on those who have a chance of doing the deal. Ultimately, the mortgage broker has to do his or her job, such pulling the credit and getting a loan application, but you must understand how to do the initial screening by *asking questions*.

Simple questions to determine a potential buyer's credit worthiness would be as follows: What you do for work? How much cash are you working with? Ever have any serious credit issues? This process will give you a quick snapshot of who you are talking to. This information must be verified by the mortgage broker, but asking these questions could save you time. Another advantage: Loan programs can be fit to your specific parameters.

How do most people buy properties that cannot be financed through the conventional path? The answer is Hard Money and Private Money.

Hard money loans are often best for short-term financing. Hard money comes from investors who strictly lend to investors needing loans on properties in need of serious renovation.

Let's look at some of the ways to find these lenders:

1. Join a local real estate investment club.

These clubs usually meet monthly, and those in attendance are involved in real estate in some form. You may have buyers, sellers, contractors, lenders, appraisers, and those who sell information services to real estate investors.

2. Network with other investors

Investors know lenders. Track every lead you find from ads or calls that you make and simply ask each one if they know any hard money lenders you might work with. As with your selling techniques, ask a lot of questions! Build your Rolodex!

3. Run ads in the newspapers that you are an investor seeking lenders (and look for ads the lenders themselves may run). Don't be shy. Run classifieds such as: "professional real estate investor seeks hard money lenders for ongoing projects."

4. Search the Internet for lenders in your area

You may go to Google or Yahoo and enter in the keywords "hard money lenders" and then add your state.

5. Contact traditional lenders to see if they have hard money programs (sometimes called "bridge loans").

6. Contact mortgage brokers and tell them that you're an investor seeking hard money lenders. Mortgage brokers broker money from many lenders, and those lenders are constantly soliciting the brokers with their various programs.

7. Check with your state business licensing boards for a list of licensed lenders.

8. View (online) your state's business regulatory site and search for lenders.

9. Visit national and regional real estate shows and conventions. Every year, there are hundreds of "shows" or conventions geared toward the real estate business.

It can be tough to find the money you need to buy investment properties. Very few people pay cash for properties; if you have it, great, but most investors need to go out and find lenders.

Of course, there are some disadvantages to nonconventional lending: high interest rates, from 12% all the way to 18%. (Note: To the average person, this sounds high, right? Yet if you account for this rate before you purchase the property and you still are making money, does it matter?) Usually, these types of loans are short-term (one year or so) and interest-only, with a "balloon" payment of the original loan amount due at the end of the term. The lender's main security is more the property than the borrower (although the lender still looks at the borrower). The lender typically prefers loans with low "LTV" (loan-to-value) ratio, usually 50% to 70% of the market value, not purchase price, whereas conventional lenders can be much more aggressive about lending on the purchase price.

Some advantages: There is a lot less red tape, and buyers can close on property in "as-is" condition. A hard money lender can also close quickly and that can help strengthen your position as a buyer when you are competing against other buyers. Hard money lenders will lend on a property that needs work, whereas a conventional lender will not. This way of financing is very common among investors across the country. As you will shortly see, hard money lenders, depending on their relationship with the borrower, sometimes lend 100% of the purchase price and may even lend for some renovation expenses.

Licensed Real Estate Agent Hat

I am a licensed real estate broker. There are some advantages to this. When I got out of collage and started to educate myself about the business while working part-time to pay my bills, going to real estate school helped fill in the gaps of basic real estate knowledge. Naturally, I also ended up with a real estate license that would make me thousands over the years, as you'll see. For any investor, there are many benefits to becoming a licensed agent and a few disadvantages, too, which I'll explain. But overall, I think getting your license is a good idea. You decide if it's right for you.

The first advantages come with the licensing process. Yes, you must pass a state test to get your license, but I consider this one of the strongest advantages. In order to pass the test, you must study; not always exciting, but you will gain a world of knowledge about real estate. The whole course is assembled and administered by folks with years of experience. Your own studies, some of which I have guided you toward already, may focus more on the creative, the marketing, renovations, and the like, while the Realtor course will focus on the specifics and legalities of real estate transactions.

So you can take the course and learn what "disclosure" requirements are (what, for instance, a seller must disclose to a prospective buyer before the sale is completed), what types of environmental hazards (radon, asbestos, mold) are regulated by state or federal law, how closings are done, and much more.

(Note: Most states will now allow you to take the real estate agent course without any "sponsorship" from a broker. A broker is responsible for regulatory oversight and the overall duties of any agent under his or her watch, while an agent is responsible only for his or her own sales and listings.)

You will also have the opportunity to save money on commissions. When a seller wants to sell a property through an agent, the agent and broker will get a percentage of the sale as their compensation. This is typically 6%, but it can often be negotiable. Sometimes the listing agent—that is, the Realtor who "lists" the property for sale—may also be the one who sells the property. Here, the agent collects the entire 6%. Other times, another agent may sell the property and so is called the "buyer's agent"; in this case, the 6% is split equally, so a $100,000 sale would produce a $6,000 commission, with $3,000 going to the listing agent and $3,000 to the selling agent.

The Motivational Hat

Real estate is hard work, make no mistake. Success comes to those who stick to it, won't take no for an answer, and, most importantly, to those who dedicate themselves to a lifetime of study and learning.

The business of real estate is comprehensive. Most people don't take the time to learn, and keep on learning, about the industry. So if you make a decision to get involved, you must make a commitment to becoming a perpetual student. Even after you learn the basics, the education process never ends because the real estate business is complex and ever-changing. When I made the decision to make this business part of my life, I committed to absorbing all the knowledge that I could get my hands on. A lot of people make decisions to do things in life, but how many of us actually make a quality commitment toward any future goals?

Find a way to enjoy the climb

"Success is a journey, not a destination." You must learn to enjoy the climb in the never-ending journey to success, because when you think you have arrived you are really going backward. I meet lots of people who are negative about what they do; to them, "job" is a negative term. Think about it: You spend most of your time working, and if you are going to be negative in this part of your life, the result is a lifetime of negativity. That is definitely not the way I want to live my life or, I believe, the way you should live yours. Regardless of what you do, you need to find a way to enjoy your work. We all have certain aspects of what we do that we don't enjoy, but we need to find some pleasure in the majority of our day-to-day duties.
Look for aspects of real investing that best suit you

This book describes how to buy and sell or rent real estate, but there are many ways of getting involved in this business. Once you understand the basics of the business, you must make sure you find a niche that makes you the happiest. You may just enjoy flipping properties and want nothing to do with property rentals. You may enjoy dealing with tenants and don't want to sell anything. You want to make sure you maximize your personal talents and have a feel for what best suits your ability to do this business most efficiently.

At some point, it's about taking action

During my professional career, I have met a lot of people who are just getting ready to get ready, waiting for their ducks to line up before they make a move. Let me tell you something—ducks don't line up, they just sit around. It's very important to have a good plan and a good strategy for your future, but without taking action, planning is useless. Likewise, "Working Smart" is very important, but taking action is vital. In this book, I talk about urgency, being aggressive, and *taking action*. These are words that I live by, and I hope that you will, too.

Finish what you start and see it ALL THE WAY THROUGH!

If you made a decision to start something, there was a reason for it. Perhaps there was a need in your life: you needed more money, wanted to leave your job, want additional income, or were seeking financial independence. A decision to make a change is the first step toward solution to your problem. But if you don't finish what you start, all the effort and time you put in initially go by the wayside, and a few years down the road you will have to start again.

Time simply cannot be wasted

Every time I try to work with a new person, I ask the same question: What is your biggest asset? I get answers like "my brain," or "my ability to communicate with people," or "my reading skills." All are attributes that any one particular person may be proud of. Yet it's rare that I get the answer I am looking for: TIME. Time is your biggest asset. You need to protect it, you need to cherish and appreciate it, especially in the real estate business, because you don't punch a time clock. *You* are the one who controls your time, because most real estate professionals are not salaried. They get paid only when a deal closes, so respecting time becomes even more crucial. Even though you are your own boss, you need to treat it like a job. Be the toughest boss you could ever have, and you'll be the wealthiest employee.

The one thing that seems to escape most people is how to do things in order of priority. Being a real estate investor means balancing a lot of different hats, but all are geared toward closing a sale (which to you means "payday"). Once you have a better understanding of the business, prioritizing becomes essential. You can be busy doing lots of things but without profitable results. You need to prioritize your tasks; this is an important aspect of being efficient and not wasting time. Look around you: Sometimes you see people working really hard with very little results. But sometimes you see people working a very light workload, but producing much greater results—these are the people who understand the order of priority and maximize their work efforts.

People Skills

To prosper in the real estate business, you should enjoy, or at least learn to enjoy, working with people. This is a people business. Not only do you need to learn the technical aspects of real estate, but you also need to become a student of your fellow human beings, developing your communication skills, your ability to persuade people, your ability to get people to like you. You will improve your success in this business and in your personal life. Of course, there are all kinds of personalities and philosophies out there. The more you are able to understand and adapt to different outlooks and views and attitudes, the easier a time you're going to have. You need to learn to persuade people when necessary, and that is not something you are necessarily born with. The real estate business involves constant interaction with many people from many walks of life. Your ability to communicate with all types will serve you for a lifetime. For example, on any given day, you may talk to a renter with a plumbing problem, a wealthy person who is selling an investment property, a lawyer with whom you must negotiate a probate sale, a title company representative who has found an old lien on your property, a cranky old contractor who needs to rebuild a kitchen for you, and many more. Be firm yet flexible, and speak clearly without talking down to people. You need to learn how to step on someone's shoes and not ruin their shine.

When I was still in college, I realized the importance of possessing people skills. I learned all I could. My ability to be flexible and easy-going, my ability to communicate with other people, and all the techniques that help me get what I want to get out of people are some of the reasons I'm successful and continue to be successful. Learn all you can about dealing with people, too!

Property Management Hat

One of the advantages of real estate is "passive income," which means making money with very little time invested. Purchasing a home and then renting it out is a great way to build wealth. You'll want to master the art of renting real estate and earning your own passive income. So let's examine our property management hat.

When I started out, I rented and managed my own properties, mainly because at that time I had no real job (just odd jobs at night). Since then, I have accumulated many rental properties and have passed all the day-to-day duties to a professional management company. With that in mind, if you already have a full-time job and real estate is something you need to pursue part-time, you may want to think about hiring a management company to handle all the duties that I will be discussing. But even if you do hire a company to take care of the day-to-day management of your rental properties, you should still be knowledgeable enough to properly screen and oversee the property management company.

Let's imagine you purchased a property and intend to rent it out—now what? The first step is to determine the rental amount. I like using my local Realtor for this information. I also drive around the neighborhood looking for "for rent" signs, and then call to determine asking prices.

Second, and not least, you'll need to find a tenant! I immediately place a sign in front of the property. This simple act is the most effective way to find a tenant. As you may have guessed, at the same time I run an ad in the local newspaper. Using the services of local Realtors to list your property for rent is another way.

Once you find a tenant, you will want to properly screen him or her. Unfortunately, I found out the hard way that having no tenant at all is preferable to getting saddled with a bad tenant. Most new investors are so impatient to find a tenant that they will rent to anyone who can fog a mirror. Bad idea. Be patient! When I speak to a potential tenant, I ask questions. Where do you live now? How much do you spend for rent currently? What do you do for a living? Who else will live with you? How long have you been at your job? This allows me (the investor) to get a good feel for whom I am speaking to. That way I don't waste my time, and I prevent countless future headaches.

So, once you have found a tenant, what is the next step? Do a background check, including a credit check. Don't leave anything to chance. There are companies on the Internet that, for a fee (I usually charge the tenant), perform background checks. For instance, in my experience, tenants in the middle of an eviction process won't disclose that information. So don't fall short screening your tenants; it will save you a lot of aggravation and money.

Once you have selected a tenant, then it's time to write up a lease and get your first month's rent, last month's rent, security deposit, and then move the tenant in. If you need a lease, depending on the market you are in, you can usually get the form from your local Realtor or an office supply store.

Now you are officially a landlord. Congratulations! I like to do my best to establish a good line of communication right from the start of my relationship with my tenants. I like to have a nice first conversation, and it goes something like this: "I want us to have a nice relationship; if things come up that need attention, please let me know, and I will call someone to take care of it." It's important to set a level of expectation with the tenants. The reality is that things do come up, regardless of how hard you try to avoid it. The most important part of being a landlord is a constant line of communication with your tenants. Without communication, it's hard to get anything done. If you find a solid tenant who takes good care of your property and pays on time, then do your best to hold on to that tenant. Get him or her a nice holiday basket; appreciate your tenant, and your tenant will appreciate you as well. Remember, your tenant is paying your mortgage and may be providing you with a nice positive cash flow.

Now, what if the tenant stops paying rent and won't respond to your requests for payment and won't cooperate to work things out? What if the tenant cuts that line of communication? Then we are left no choice but to start an eviction proceeding. That is the process of removing a tenant from your property through the courts. Not a good situation, but a necessary one to get your property back and rent to someone who will pay as promised. Depending on your location, check with your local county for the process. If you are looking to be a landlord, keep in mind that evictions, vacancies, and maintenance are all part of the rental business, and as long as you are prepared for this both mentally and financially, you should be okay. On a personal note: Having many rental properties myself, dealing with the above negative issues on a regular basis is much better than the RAT RACE.

For more tools about the information in this section, visit my website at www.TheRoadToRealEstateWealth.com.

Part Two:
Case Studies in Real Estate

My First Deal!
How I Purchased My First Property with No Money and Made $5,500

Case Study One

It was during my last year of college that the real estate bug bit me.

I will share with you the moment that everything coalesced in my mind, and I made that crucial decision to take the most important step in any journey—the first step.

The notion of being a real estate investor had been rattling around in my mind for some time. Perhaps this notion occurs to many people, but most don't follow through. There are many ways to become involved in real estate, but I wanted to be an investor. Being an investor, to me, means to be a principal and an owner of real estate. I wanted to build wealth and establish passive income; that was the only part that interested me. Despite being in the business for years now and completing many deals, my view of the process has not changed, and the aspirations that were clear to me then remain clear to me now. I know more, and the processes have grown more sophisticated, but I never waver on the final goal.

With less than a year until graduation, I was sitting around just yakking with a friend of mine who lived in the same apartment complex that I lived in near school. We had just gotten back from playing some hoops, one-on-one basketball that was great for blowing off steam after school. Somehow we got to talking about the apartment complex. My friend mentioned that he owned his unit. I thought that was great. Though he had a few years on me, he seemed quite young to have already bought real estate.

I asked when he had bought it (a few years before), how much he paid, and how much his mortgage cost him, and he said the mortgage was $550 per month. Now, understand: I was paying $800 month in rent for a unit identical to one my buddy owned for only for $550 a month. I was just renting, with no possible equity accumulation. My landlord was what you call an "absentee" owner, who paid a Realtor to rent out and manage the property.

This was the moment. A light snapped on above my head, and my stomach tightened. I knew I was going to get involved in the real estate business. The title "real estate investor" just came to mind, in full view.

The absentee owner was earning $200 a month, and except for making a few phone calls now and then, he invested little time on a day-to-day basis. That's what I wanted. Who wouldn't?

It would take me more than 18 months before I bought my first property. I needed to build a foundation of knowledge, to learn about and find financing ideas, before I stepped up and inked my first deal. During the next year and a half, I started putting together the building blocks of knowledge in preparation for what would lie ahead.

During those formative days, I finished college and desperately looked for employment. I had a finance degree, but it didn't seem to help much. I was told I was over-qualified for entry-level positions and under-qualified for more advanced positions. Frustrated, I accepted "temp work," the type where you sort of have a job, but it doesn't last, and you don't really work long at any one place. I was struggling. Credit cards were a considerable part of my day-to-day finances, with me sometimes borrowing from one to pay another, but they served a part of my plan: to build my up my credit.

These cards would soon do more, as you'll see shortly. I attended every real estate course possible: the workshops, the multiple-day courses. (I had taken only one real estate course in college.) I read dozens of books. I ordered packaged courses from nearly every decent real estate infomercial I caught on television. Even then, when money was tight and every penny counted, I realized that spending on the most important part of my body—my brain—would one day pay off with huge dividends.

Despite my struggles, I continued to invest time and effort to learn the real estate business; I never took my eye off the big picture, the long-term view. Without those images pressed in my brain, I would never have had the determination to make the deals I was about to make.

From time to time, as I accumulated knowledge, I experimented with different techniques and philosophies that I had studied. (Even with a long-term view, I was anxious to get in the game!) Not much success. My early false starts were, of course, due in large part to my lack of experience and my still murky knowledge of the real estate game and how winners play it. I still lacked confidence. I hadn't put sufficient time in yet or had the victories that would bring me the necessary confidence. Finally, of course, I had no money! So, I asked for no money down. I even asked the seller to pay the closing costs and defer the payments. I tried all the no-money-down course ideas I'd studied, but I attempted to leverage the seller to the point that my offers were so pitifully weak no seller would ever go for them.

The bottom line is, when you are new at this, not sure in your knowledge, have empty pockets, and have yet to find the successes that will prop up your confidence level, you will try to compensate by being overly conservative in every aspect of your deal. So I made very low offers (too low to be realistic), overestimated my renovation costs, and put such "buyer-biased" language in my contracts that I made it impossible for even the most desperate seller to accept them.

Remember those credit card payments I was juggling? One course that I took was an aggressive, "not-a-dime-down" kind of presentation. They spoke about using your credit cards to get started buying real estate. They said credit cards have some cash value, that some or all of our credit lines can be applied to get cash. So per the instructor's direction, I created a list of credit card companies and applied to everyone I could. I had no home to refinance or use for an equity line of credit. No bank would give me a loan on my signature alone. The only way I saw to get the capital for my first property—

interest rates on the cards be damned—was by using credit card money. Kind of spooky, huh? I thought so, too. But, as you must be, I was determined to make my dream happen.

I sat down one morning at 9 a.m. and did not stop applying for cards until four in the afternoon. I sent in 30 different applications. Realize that up to that point I had only one card—with a $500 limit. Luckily, I had paid on time and had a clean, if brief, credit history. This paid off. I ended up with a total of $33,000 in credit card cash advance power.

I started poring through the local newspapers in search of good leads, just as I had learned in my training courses. (To this day, I still use newspapers to find many of my investment leads.) I learned to look for keywords that sellers use, things like "handyman special," or "must sell," or "in probate," or "make offer," or "priced to sell fast." Any clues that hint at distress signals.

I was a non-stop classified reader. I soon learned, as every successful person must, that you must press on, be relentless, and not give up. Most people give up when they are on the brink of victory. I didn't, and don't you!

And, indeed, the day finally came that I spotted the ad that would change my life. The ad matched my image of "investment property." The ad said the property was an estate sale, fresh out of probate. (Probate is a court process used for people who pass away without a will; the courts assign a representative who ensures that the property can be sold without any problems with title.) I called and found my first deal.

The sellers told me that they were due to close on the property in three weeks. If they could find a buyer who could come through before their close, they would be willing to wholesale the property and cut a great deal.

Excited, I traveled over to see the property. It was a nice two-bedroom, two-bath condo. The complex was huge, with many two-story buildings. The 1,100-square-foot unit I was interested in was on the second floor. It required little work, which was a considerable plus, especially for my first buy. It even had some furniture that they would leave behind—I was fresh out of college, I wasn't choosy about furniture! The sellers said they would accept $33,000 if I could come up with the money fast.

I went to work completing my research. First, I found comps (other closed sales to help me determine the true market value); I got this information through a Realtor whom I had been dealing with. I found eight different closed sales in the complex within the last three to six months that were the same size and floor plan. The value was $55,000. I also looked at the amount of work the unit needed and determined the renovations to be only about $1,500. (I only needed to change the carpet and paint the unit.) Keep in mind that you do need money to invest in real estate, but having the knowledge and ability to recognize good deals from bad ones, I believe, is just as important. I went to my bank and got friendly with one of the loan officers, who told me that the bank would typically lend about 75% of the market value on this type of condo. Now, you know I couldn't yet qualify for a loan, so why even ask? Again, this is an example of my studying paying off. As discussed earlier, financing is everything in real estate. So I put on my mortgage broker/banker hat on before I even made an offer on this condo. You see, I had the cash advance on credit cards available to purchase the property, but as we all know, at an 18% to 22% interest rate, it might not be the best long-term financing option. Therefore, I did my homework on the requirements of refinancing before I even made my offer. I was putting a strategy into place, as you'll soon see.

So, where was I? I offered the seller $28,000 (remember, he was asking $33,000) and we settled on $30,000. I needed $30,000 for the purchase, plus another $1,000 in closing costs. I had that much available from the credit card cash line I had built up. I was comfortable with the property and very comfortable with the price I was paying. Still, it was my first property investment and a nerve-wracking decision. The fear that most people have of crossing that path—from talking about doing it to actually doing it—was right in front of me. Honestly, it is not easy to take that first step. Everything that can go wrong, real or imagined, churned through my head, as it will yours when you first go for it. This was it, though. I got on the telephone, nervously dialing each credit card issuer to begin the cash advance process. It took me about a week and a half to get the money over to my checking account.

I calculated the interest costs on the $31,000 would come to roughly $800 month; even with high interest rates, credit cards generally require only a small monthly minimum payment. I quickly realized that this was the same amount that I was paying in rent, but now I was going to be an owner!

Before long, I had gathered all the money in my bank account. I took it back out in the form of a cashier's check and drove to the title company for the closing. Now, I was a homeowner of a condo in Florida at the age of 23.

Once I got over the initial excitement of owning my very first investment property, it was time to put the next stage of my strategy into play.

Remember a few pages back, when I had gone to the bank to inquire about a "refinance?" I returned to my bank and applied for a loan for 70% of the value of my new condo. This totaled $38,000. To date, I had invested about $32,500 in the property, including closing costs, minor renovations, and interest. Three weeks after my application to refinance and only five weeks after I purchased the condo, I closed on my new loan. The bank handed me a check for $37,500(the loan amount was $38,000 less $500 in closing costs). I paid off my credit cards and pocketed $5,500. As you can imagine, I was thrilled. I looked forward to building on this positive experience. And I realized that while money was still vital, knowledge is the most priceless commodity.

I ended up living in the condo for the next year. My mortgage payment was $700. I rented a room to a buddy for $400 a month. So not only had I put no money into the property, but I pocketed $5,500 and reduced my monthly expense for shelter from $700 a month to only $300 a month.

To this day, I still own and rent out that first condo. Since I bought it, it has more than doubled in value and has produced a steady cash flow. You know how some people say, "If I did it, so can you?" Well, I did it. And so can you.

Case Study Two

How I Risked $5,000 in Credit Card Money and Made $20,000

After doing my first deal ever, I had a sense of urgency and eagerness to find another good deal and continue my positive momentum. Since I was still very new to this business, my Rolodex was extremely skinny, and I was working on developing contacts to help me. After doing my first deal, I realized that finding the right investment and having the right knowledge to back it up are the keys to being successful in this business. Nonetheless, finding money remains the biggest challenge for a new or current investor, as it was for me.

My next deal was two separate duplexes; one duplex had one bedroom and one bath on one side of the unit, and another had one bedroom and one bath on the other side of the building. It was a one-story structure. The other duplex was right next door and featured an identical floor plan. I had gathered this lead from a previous contact I made. As I mentioned earlier, keeping good records of people you speak to on a regular basis, be they buyers or sellers, is vital. With the computer technology now available to us, you might say that these days it's easier, cheaper, and more efficient to reach more people.

I keep the name and number of every worthwhile person I speak to in this business. During my daily follow-up calls to my potential sellers, I spoke to one particular investor who had purchased two duplexes from the courthouse at a foreclosure auction sale and now was looking to wholesale these two deals in "as-is" condition. (Foreclosures are a good source, but it's a complex area for a new investor with little experience or a lack of cash. You need to be sophisticated and have an understanding of the foreclosure process, and you must understand how the city works in regard to violations, lien positions, and foreclosure sales in regard to any debt owed. You'll need to know what you, as a new property owner, will be responsible for and what you will not be responsible for.) A good way to find properties is to network with other investors. Going to the courthouse may not be a good option for a new investor to purchase properties, but attending the sale at the courthouse will help you to develop contacts. Remember, the people attending these auctions are investors just like you. A good percentage of these investors are probably looking to flip the properties (wholesale). Perhaps there are lenders attending these auctions looking to develop new perspective borrowers. Bottom line: Even if you have no intention of making a bid, attending these auctions, I believe, will provide a great source of networking.

This particular investor who had these two duplexes for sale was an experienced investor who had been in the industry for a while and was a regular at these auctions. I still had very little money and had yet to really establish myself with hard money lenders. What had allowed me to do my first deal were credit cards and the ability to pull cash from them. My only real source of cash at this point was still those credit cards. I knew that was not something I could continue; credit cards were not an ideal long-term solution to my acquisition needs, merely an entrée into the game.

After speaking to this seller (investor), I took down some information, and I went to work. After a year and a half of studying this business, I was learning to distinguish between good deals and bad deals. I learned to recognize and analyze what would be a good potential investment.

I quickly took down the address and asked questions, such as, "Is the property rented?" (In this case, only one side of each duplex was rented.) The investor had just purchased these properties from a foreclosure sale, so he was both the owner and the seller for this particular deal. That same day, I drove to see the properties. This was a blue-collar neighborhood with a mixture of multi-family and single-family homes. The properties were next to a major interstate. A good way to analyze properties when they are tenant-occupied is to try to speak to the tenants and ask them questions. I asked, "How long have you lived here?" and "Are there any problems with the property?" Remember that negative information spreads faster than positive information. Tenants tend to talk about anything that is wrong where they live, in hopes that someone will improve the property. So take that into account.

The properties were not in the greatest shape. Since the previous owner was the bank, very little had been done with ongoing maintenance and property management. The current owner/investor had no intention of keeping this property or managing it. This particular investor purchased properties from the courthouse steps in foreclosure auctions and planned on wholesaling these properties at a discounted price to another investor. One reason the investor did this was because he paid such low prices that he could sell to another investor, leaving him room to make money as well, and still make a satisfactory profit. This investor understood that by selling the property at a discount he was able to move more properties. The more properties he moved, the more money he made.

The seller was asking $45,000 per duplex. I looked at the tax roll and the comparable sales in the area and determined the market value to be $90,000 each. I did not have any relationships with hard money lenders or enough credit on my credit cards for a $90,000 purchase. I certainly did not have the cash in the bank to purchase these two duplexes. But I knew from my analysis, and I knew in my gut, that this particular investment was a good deal and that I could find someone who would pay more than $45,000 for each. I'm going to repeat something that I heard when I first got into this business: "Real estate is gambling with knowledge." You must have all the information available to you to make the most informed decision. There are definitely risks with real estate, but with the right knowledge, they can be calculated. When I sat down and looked at this deal, I realized it was a great one, but I still lacked the ability to attain the financing to purchase it. Remember, you can always (with the right marketing and the right deal) wholesale properties. You see, when you wholesale you don't have to rehab the property or actually purchase the property. You are selling your contract position; all you are doing is selling paper. So you don't need any money to wholesale properties, except perhaps for deposits to purchase.

This particular deal turned out to be very important to me because I knew I couldn't close the property I was about to put under contract. The seller wanted a $2,000-per-property nonrefundable deposit, not contingent on anything except to close the property within a 30-day time frame. That meant I needed to put up $4,000 and had 30 days to either purchase both duplexes for $90,000 or find another buyer willing to pay more than $45,000 per duplex and assign my contract to them. If I could not have all this accomplished within the 30-day period, I would lose $4,000. At that time in my life, to lose $4,000 would have meant major disaster and could have even discouraged me from any further activity in this industry. I did not even have $4,000 to spare in my bank account. I made a decision to cash-advance the deposit money from my credit cards. I wrote up the contract, gave the seller $4,000, and made a decision to move forward and tie up these two duplexes.

The first thing I did was run a newspaper ad that specifically targeted investors. Not only did I need to find a buyer within the next 30 days, but I also needed to find a buyer who would be able to close within the time frame that had been allocated to me (by agreement in the contract). I knew in my heart that I had put two good properties under contract and that they had a lot of marketability. I had found two nice duplexes that were next to each another; this would make it more attractive to an investor from a management perspective, as side-by-side units are effective to manage. They had good curb appeal; they were in a popular, centrally-located investment area. So there were a lot of favorable things going for this property. I had no doubt that there was somebody out there who would soon recognize the value I had found in this property.

So I ran an ad in the local newspaper and listed the duplexes for $59,900 each. The ad was very investor-specific, with words like, "great investment" and "priced below market." I was hopeful and optimistic that I would attract the kind of buyer who would fit this particular property. One might say that I put quite a bit of pressure on myself, but there comes a time when you must trust your knowledge and ability, find the confidence within yourself, and just do it. This was such a moment. I knew that finding a buyer was just half the battle; I needed a buyer who would have the ability to close as well.

I started getting calls, and sent the potential buyers to look at the properties and followed up as best as I could.

There was one buyer who professed keen interest. He had driven by the properties and seemed very interested. The prospect was a full-time chef who was looking to diversify his income. At this point, I was one week into my four-and-a-half-week closing deadline. The potential buyer told me he was interested at an asking price of $59,000 per duplex. After the buyer did his due diligence, he offered me $57,000 per duplex, and I was excited about that offer. The next morning, I was supposed to get together with the buyer to write a contract and get a deposit. (I always try to get a deposit amount identical to what I had put up; in this case I had put up $2,000 per duplex, so I was asking for a $2,000 deposit per duplex from the buyer.)

Unfortunately, instead of a meeting time, I got a message from the buyer saying he was no longer interested. That could have been it, and I might have just continued marketing. But something told me this guy was the right one for the property. I did not give up, and called him despite his "not interested" message. I wanted to find out the real reason for his change of heart. I felt that he really liked it, that he was the right buyer, and that he wanted to make that tough decision to buy. So I called him, and learned that his brother-in-law had given him negative advice (ever had that happen to you?). Knowing what was at stake for me, I had to try to build trust by applying the sales skills that I had been studying.

Luckily for me, I talked him off the fence and got him back and interested in the properties. You must understand: Most people are scared and nervous when making a decision about something new to them. You need to be patient and use the consultative selling method that we discussed earlier. In this particular sale, I educated the buyer as well as sold him. When you're dealing with new buyers, you need to understand that they have very little knowledge, and they need to trust the person on the other side of the transaction. Part of selling to a new person is not only the trust aspect; it is also the education part of it. You see, you need to educate and sell at the same time. This is why having extensive knowledge in what you do is very important, especially in the real estate business. When you are able to express yourself with clarity and confidence, those attributes will greatly improve your closing ability. Understanding this will certainly bring you better sales results.

Having secured a contract to close at the same time as my original closing, I also received the same amount of deposit that I had put up, which in turn I made nonrefundable to my buyer. At least at this point, if my buyer couldn't come through, I would not lose my deposit with the original seller. Be that as it may, I was in this business to make a profit, not just protect a deposit. So now my focus was to make sure that my buyer was able to obtain financing. At this point, I had about three weeks left before my deadline to close. My buyer, the chef, was trying to obtain conventional bank financing to purchase these two duplexes. We did not have a lot of time. So this deal was now in the hands of the mortgage broker and the buyer. All I could do at this point was to try to efficiently follow up with the buyer, mortgage broker, title company, and anybody else involved in this transaction.

As the deadline closed in, I realized my buyer would not be able to close within that time frame. My original contract with the seller was at risk of being voided. One thing you need to understand when you're dealing with experienced investors (such as my duplex seller)is they are sharp; they know what they're doing. Just as I have been preaching to you, they try to maximize the profits on every deal. Having said that, I approached the seller in hopes of extending my closing deadline. The seller did not want to extend the deadline for my contract. I had a problem.

So my only choice was to offer the seller more money in exchange for extending the contract. Here was a classic example of a savvy contract from a savvy investor. I had to offer the seller an additional $2,000 per duplex for a two-week extension. Had I not done so, I would have no profit. So instead of making $24,000, I made $20,000, which is a still great circumstance to be in. And what I learned here is that I should have had an option to pay for an extension of the closing date, rather than having to negotiate it at the last moment. Just as I mentioned earlier in the hats analogy, everything written in that contract is what you have to live up to. As you get more experienced, and as you do more deals in the real estate business, you come to realize the importance of a properly written contract.

The outcome of this transaction left me exhilarated. I had come to realize the purpose of my hard work and had seen all my efforts come to fruition. And I was just getting started. I still had a lot of challenges and much room to grow and learn. My buyer the chef became a good friend of mine, and a person I continued to do business with for years to come. When I received the message that he was not interested, I could have torn up the message and given up on that specific contact, but I chose not to. You need to approach this business with the mentality that it's not over till it's over. This deal was an important one for my career because it developed certain contacts for me, from the new buyer to the seller to the new mortgage broker, and this created a good list of professionals who could help me in my business. And to think that if I had not been persistent, and had failed to pursue the chef, I could've lost out on lots of future profits.

Here are some lessons from this transaction:

Market Aggressively and Quickly

Real estate is not a cash business or retail business. Once you find a deal and put it under contract, no one else can legally buy that property without your approval. You have a certain time frame, before closing, that you are in control of the real estate; you don't own it, but you have rights to it. During that time, it's a brilliant thing to find a buyer and make a profit before or at the time of the deadline on your existing contract.

Even if your intention was to close on it, which for most people is the only thing they know or understand, why not wholesale at a profit as soon as possible, even before you close? Part of the advantage to someone buying from you, in this scenario, is he or she can save on closing costs, as you as seller may not have even paid closing costs yourself (you haven't closed, right?).

Why do so many investors wait till the last minute to begin to market their properties? Now you know that, from the very first day you have the property under contract, you can start to market and "sell" that property. Everything in business seems to take longer than we estimate it will take, so giving yourself this time advantage can make or break a deal.

Putting myself in the buyer's shoes, every time I find a potential seller who is trying to flip a property that he or she still has under contract, I know I can make a good deal, because the seller is motivated. So, don't wait! The moment you have a property under contract, begin to aggressively market the property there and then.

Close more deals by maintaining and tracking your leads better than the other guy.

I found this property because I kept my leads organized and available to me on a consistent basis. Most people call their current leads a few times and then follow up only monthly or even end up throwing valuable leads away. Early on, I made a commitment to get every possible dollar out of my leads, so I followed up religiously and consistently. Do the same: Track the database of leads you develop, track each follow-up contact you make, and make certain you don't give up on that lead until that person tells you he or she is no longer interested in any real estate deals. Until then, you don't stop!

Good sales skills can make the difference. Remember, my buyer, after showing strong interest in this deal when first we spoke, suddenly turned 180 degrees and left me an abrupt message that he was no longer going to consider buying the property. How did I turn this around and make a success of it? It was my belief in what I do and my commitment that, when shared with him, made all the difference. Further, it was my use of classic sales skills. I probed and found the specific objection he had (communicated to him by his brother-in-law): he worried that the neighborhood was too blue collar and this would hold down the real estate values.

Here's how I handled it: so many people take advice from others who have no knowledge of the subject matter. Since I offered the property at a great price, I simply stated the facts; in this case, showing him what similar properties were worth (much more) and letting him know that neighborhoods can appreciate, relative to the value around them. Also, I worked hard to develop his trust, just being a straight-shooter; that is enough to move many people off the fence.

Don't Give Up!

Sound trite? Perhaps you've heard "Don't give up" so often you think it's nothing. But it is nearly everything.

And the phrase means different things for different people. For my younger cousin, it meant that he would not quit our late-night checkers-playing session until HE won—on the 10th game of the evening!

For me, the most vital part of the story is that I did not give up easily on a lead who said flatly he was not interested. I didn't take rejection personally; I knew it was "just business." So I picked up the phone and turned a dead lead into a profitable sale. More than that, this deal was instrumental in cementing my career. And my buyer became an important partner in many future deals.

Case Study Three

Building, Networking, and Partnering with People You Meet

Once I sold my two duplexes to the new investor from my previous deal, I developed a relationship with my buyer that led in turn to a partnership. When you are selling anything, especially real estate, people need to trust you. Without trust, no one will want to do business with you. Meeting with folks who have money should be in your weekly schedule. It's in my weekly schedule because it's so important. It's just as important as buying, marketing, selling, etc. So after I sold the two duplexes to my new buyer, we developed a friendship and a level of trust that led me to stage two of my learning process.

My first deal was done with all credit cards; my second deal was done with credit cards for deposit and a simultaneous flip (this meant I still did not have to use my own money or try to get a hard money lender to help me, which would mean money out of my pocket). But I still had to develop capital resources and private lender relationships (which can only be established over time by actually doing deals, using some capital and recycling loans). But one thing I did have was a lot of knowledge, some level of experience, and a good amount of confidence. You are about to undertake a business that requires knowledge and capital. So you need to use every advantage you can. In my case, my partner the chef was someone who had capital (at least, more than me) but limited knowledge and a full-time job. He had a strong desire to get involved in the business and diversify his income, but with only a limited amount of time. So after a few conversations, we both came to the conclusion that we may have a possible "marriage." With my time, knowledge, and his financial support, we might help each other in the common quest of becoming substantial real estate investors.

When I purchased my first deal, I kept in contact with the seller, who was an investor as well. You see, once you establish a legitimate contact, you must stay in touch with that individual and try to network with him or her. It's very important to work with people who know and understand what you are looking for. This includes appraisers, mortgage brokers, title companies, contractors, sellers, and buyers. Let me give you an example.

If you're shopping for a shirt and you ask the salesperson for help, and he or she steers you into the underwear section, you get frustrated pretty fast.

The same holds in this business when you are dealing with your support team. As you develop your contacts, you must make certain that they are comfortable and prepared to deal with an investor's atmosphere. It's fast, it's aggressive, and you need to be on the same channel.

I called the investor I purchased my first deal from and asked if he had any properties for sale. He sent me via fax a list of different homes. One home was a two-bedroom, one-bath single-family home with an asking price of $69,000, and another was a three-bedroom, two-bath single-family home with an asking price of $79,000. Since the seller was someone who wholesaled real estate, his homes were priced right for investors.

With my new partner in place, I now could put myself in a position to improve my buying power (even though my partner did not have cash for the properties, he had the down payment and renovation money, which was more than I had).

Why did I partner up? Sometimes it's better to have 50% of something big than 100% of something smaller, or even worse, 100% of zero. Even though I wanted to become a success through my own initiative, every successful businessperson needs help or partners in some form. Through the strength of the team, we can often accomplish much more than we can by struggling alone. The fact is, there are very few real "self-made" successes out there.

I looked at both homes: The first home was small (two

bedrooms, one bathroom, and only 600 sq. ft.), but it was on a large lot. They were asking $69,000. The second home was larger (three bedrooms, two bathrooms, 1,200 sq. ft). The asking price for the second home was $79,000.

I called a Realtor I know and asked for closed sales on the two-bedroom home (remember to compare "apples to apples" and make sure all the variables such as lot size, square footage, and year built are similar). I gathered these comparables and concluded that this small, "2/1" was worth $130,000. I did the same research on the bigger home and found the value to be nearly $150,000. So, based on the asking price and market value, it seemed that we had something here.

Now that the deal looked good on paper, it warranted a trip to view the property. Once on site, I immediately noticed the two homes were close in proximity. That was a nice plus. As I had driven to the first home, I did as I always do: I took notice of the neighborhood, its condition, and how meticulous residents were about upkeep. The first home featured an attractive, large corner lot, even though the home was very small. A huge tree stood on the property, near the back of the home but far enough away to shelter the lot without adding any risk (from roots, overhang) to the home. Most investors would have shied away because of the small size of the home—it's really unusual to find a 600 sq. ft. home—but to me, every property can be a great investment, as long as you get it at the right price and you can envision the right buyer for it. You must develop the ability to visualize potential; to do this, you must learn to "see" the property in a salable state and picture what kind of buyer you will eventually put into it.

Of course, without the numbers being right, you can visualize all you want, but you will struggle to make it work.

I had learned from picking mortgage brokers' brains that a bank underwriter (that's a person who actually approves the loan) examines not only your credit but also the property and its value, as the property is the bank's ultimate security. In this case, part of visualizing the potential buyer also required an understanding of the type of financing that this buyer would eventually have to obtain; many banks are slow to lend on small, unusual properties. So I made sure that my comparables were also 600 sq. ft. just to cover me for later when I would sell this property.

As I arrive at a potential investment, I find myself putting on multiple hats. Here, I put on my investor hat, then my contractor hat, soon my salesperson hat, and, before long, my mortgage broker hat. My thought process as I started to analyze the renovation and sale of this tiny home was to sell it to a single parent with one to two children, or even a small family with one child. In the same manner as I try to visualize a property in its later, renovated state, I also try to picture my target clients. For example, I once went to a real estate seminar where the speaker bought only oceanfront homes with values ranging from $25-35 million. Sounds crazy, right? But I learned from his lecture was that these homes were so expensive that very, <u>very</u> few people can afford them. So before he even took on a project, he would estimate how many people in the entire world could actually afford these homes. I remembered him saying that for one home he was going to build, he was able to identify only 1,500 people in the world who could actually buy the home. This is a good example of knowing who your potential clients are. You see, most people who look at his homes will love them, but how many can afford them? With my homes, most people can afford them—I just have to find buyers who love them. In this example, the "2/1," I had found an affordable home with lots of backyard playing space. So in my mind, I imagined that selling this house to an owner/occupant was the way to go.

As I walked through the house, I noticed that a new kitchen needed to be installed. The kitchen cabinets had deteriorated, the counters were made out of Formica, and the sink had mildew and appeared to not have been used for some time. As I opened the cabinet beneath the sink to get an idea of the state of the plumbing, I noticed that the base of the kitchen cabinet inside was rotting (perhaps indicating a plumbing leak).

The doors in the kitchen had been made from cheap particle board, leaving them warped and dilapidated. I would have to replace the whole kitchen, because simply to replace the doors and cabinets would not have brought the kitchen up to a level of quality that I could market with confidence.

My next stop as I moved through the house was the bathroom.

As I stepped into the bathroom, I saw the tub straight ahead; it wasn't terrible, but it looked neglected. The tile around it was intact and was not damaged or chipped, but was very grimy. The toilet was cracked at the tank, and frankly, even when it was new, it probably had been very unattractive. The vanity had been ripped out of the bathroom, so I definitely needed to install one. A good solution to the bathroom situation was to resurface the tub and the tile around it, rather than replacing these materials. Since all of this was intact, I just needed to improve it cosmetically. (Here's a good way to save money with bathrooms: there are companies out there that use a special paint to resurface tile, tubs, toilets, so instead of replacing these items you simply apply a special plastic coating, similar to that used on boats, that is very long-lasting and looks great. That saves the labor and material costs to replace these items.)

After looking at the kitchen and bathroom, I examined the windows. I always make certain that every window is operable. With the exception of two broken glass panes, the windows were in good shape.

As I examined the walls inside and out, I knew I would need to paint everything, but nearly every distressed property I buy needs paint inside and out. I try to visualize what colors would best fit the location and the home's décor, and what would attract the most attention to the property.

Luckily, the exterior walls were structurally in good shape and would not need intensive preparation prior to painting. Same with the interior; the drywall was intact, and basic painting was all that was required.

The last thing that I examined was the flooring. The kitchen, bath, and common areas had small (6" x 6") white ceramic tile, and the grout was packed with dirt and grime. The gray carpeting covering the bedroom was heavily stained to the point that it could not be cleaned and was unrecoverable.

Here are the repairs I settled on:

Kitchen: I would completely replace the kitchen, countertops, cabinets, and plumbing (including the sink and faucet). The cost would be approximately $1,200.

Bathroom: I chose to re-glaze the tub and the tiles on the wall above the tub; in addition, I would replace the toilet and install a new vanity, sink, and faucet. As this was a small bathroom, I chose a small vanity without cabinets and instead would use a "medicine cabinet" with mirror that would not have such a large footprint on the floor. My cost would run to $800.

Walls: I selected an off-white paint for the full interior; outside, I chose a brown pastel and decided to trim the outside windows in white, which would produce a clean look. Cost: $1,200.

Flooring: I would replace the small tiles with larger (12" x 12") tiles in off-white; the effect of this helped to make the home appear roomier inside. The carpet had to go, to be replaced with a light beige alternative, to help enhance the natural light inside. Here, I would spend $600 on carpet and $1,200 on tile.

Finally, some final touches, such as wall switches, a new water heater, and landscaping would run $700.

The one advantage you have when renovating a smaller property is that the material and labor costs are smaller due to the sheer fact that smaller amounts of time and material are poured into a smaller project. I estimated the renovation—everything outlined above—to be $6,350. I added $1,650 to that, which is about 20% of my estimate, as my "rainy day" fund.

The second home (three bedrooms, two baths, 1,200 sq. ft.) also needed work. This home was not on a corner lot. It had an attractive circular driveway. The house had a grayish look with blue trimming around the windows, with a pretty backyard on a very square-type lot.

This home, I thought, would best sell to someone who would live there—not an investor but specifically someone who wanted this as his or her starter home. Why? Because of that attractive backyard, for one; I knew it would be attractive to me if I was looking for a home, and so it might be attractive to others. Being a three-bedroom, and especially, having two baths, this floor plan was very family-friendly.

As I walked in the house, I entered the living room, and straight in front of me I found the kitchen. As I inspected the kitchen, I noticed that, while it wasn't particularly attractive, it was made of fine-quality solid woods. Having said that, it would provide me the opportunity to give the kitchen a facelift, changing the cabinet hardware, and tiling the wood countertop with a backsplash. I decided to change the sink and plumbing fixtures as well.

Then I proceeded to a skinny hallway that led me to three bedrooms, with a common bathroom in the hallway and another bathroom in the master bedroom. I like to use ceramic tile for all the common areas except for the bedrooms, where I prefer carpeting. The kitchen was fair. It did not need replacing, but it did need a facelift. My definition of a facelift was changing the doors, resurfacing the countertop, and changing the hinges. The house needed flooring, closet doors, painting inside and out, and a complete re-do of the bathrooms. I estimated this renovation cost at $13,000.

Going back to my acquisition formula, I didn't want to be into this for more than 70% of market value. The two-bedroom, one-bath home was valued at $130,000 so *.70 = $91,000 - $69,000 (purchase price) + $8,000(renovation) + $10,000(the closing costs and holding time), this project would cost me $87,000, which is less than the $91,000 maximum. Based on this information, the purchase price of $69,000 would work; there was definitely room to make money in this particular home.

The second home (three bedrooms, two baths, 1200 sq. ft.) worked out thus: at $150,000, 70% of that is $105,000, minus the purchase price, which in this case is $79,000, plus renovation costs ($13,000) + $11,000 for closing costs and holding time. This means the project would cost me $103,000. The numbers worked for this house as well.

After establishing my market value and my renovation costs, the decision was pretty easy. We decided to move forward and make a strong offer, nearly the asking price, in order to give ourselves the best chance to put these properties under contract. Remember: When you find a deal that makes sense, it's just a matter of time before another investor snaps up that property, and you miss an opportunity. You need to move fast, efficiently, and with a sense of urgency. When you know something is good and the asking price already makes sense, don't get greedy. I'm all for paying the lowest price, but sometimes greed can cost you the property as the seller may try to get a figure closer to the asking price. If the seller is an investor, he may have priced it for another savvy investor. As you wait for the seller to accept your lower offer, another investor can come in, offer the full asking price, and cut you out of the deal. I know different people have different personalities, but business is business. Good deals don't fall off trees, so don't hesitate when you find something special; be aggressive, do your due diligence, and make a decision.

So we made an offer for the two-bedroom, one-bath home. He was asking $69,000, and we offered an aggressive $66,000. We also offered $75,000 on the second home; he was asking $79,000 for the three-bedroom, two-bath. Since the seller owned both properties, that gave us a bit of leverage, and we were hoping for a group discount.

I believe if we had been only trying to buy one property the seller wouldn't have been as flexible. We were hoping for a break. Luckily, the seller accepted our offers, but he wanted us to close in three weeks (a shorter than conventional time in the regular real estate world, but remember you are entering the irregular real estate world). We signed the usual investor-type contract, which meant we were buying the properties in as-is condition. We did ask for a three-day inspection period. This contract was not contingent on financing, but the seller was required to provide us free and clear title. We also gave the seller a $1,500-per-property nonrefundable deposit.

Since I had yet to use a hard money lender, I was hoping my new partnership would get my foot in the door and start building my name with some of the private lenders investing in my area. As I mentioned earlier, the amount the lender is willing to lend will depend upon the relationship and trust that he has in you as the investor, in addition to how much equity you have in the property (which is ultimately a security blanket for the lender in case things go sour).

We handed over our $3,000 in combined nonrefundable deposit monies without first securing our financing—a bit risky, wouldn't you say? Most professional, savvy investors (in this case, the seller) will not tie up a property with inspections and a financing contingency (in regular real estate, it is common to have a time frame for inspections and financing). Had I asked for a financing contingency, the seller may have balked and accepted another offer instead. But he did grant me a three-day inspection period. This meant that if for any reason I was not comfortable with the amount of work the property needed I could request, in writing, a refund of my money. The bottom line? A cancellation would not cost me my $3,000 deposit as long as I gave notice of my intent to do so within three days.

During those three days of the inspection period, I worked diligently to secure my financing. And if I could not have obtained financing within these three days, we would have backed out of the deal. We are not in the business of losing deposits; this is a good example of how we put our lawyer hats on. Even though three days might not sound like a lot of time, most of the hard money lenders are well aware of the fast-paced investment atmosphere. Most will give you a yes or no decision fairly quickly, whereas in the regular real estate world it could take weeks. When you are first starting out in this business and the hard money lenders are doing a deal with you for the first time, they will be conservative and cautious. So, part of the reason that I found a partner (in this case, the chef) was to provide the closing costs, renovation, and down payment money. We sent out proposals to three different hard money lenders. A day and a half into our three-day inspection period, we started to get some replies as to how much they were willing to lend. On the two-bedroom, one-bath, we asked the hard money lender to lend the full asking price of $66,000 and closing costs, or a total of $71,000.

For the three-bedroom, two-bath that we had a contract for at $75,000, we were asking the same, full purchase price and closing costs, which amounted to $80,000. The best we could find was the full purchase price, and they wanted to lend only half my closing costs. So out of all three lenders, the highest we got for the small home was $68,500, and for the three-bedroom, two-bath only $77,500. All three hard money lenders had very similar terms; the same interest rate and the same up front points (15% plus 3 points), but the loan amount is what differed. Remember, if you send three different lenders or even three different appraisers to the same property, you will most likely get three different values. Those values might not be tremendously far apart from one another, but they will be different. Therefore, though we came to the conclusion that the two-bedroom, one-bath was worth $130,000, and we based our analysis on that value, that did not mean the lenders would agree. Always *undervalue* the property because lenders have different interests. They are more concerned about protecting their investment and hedging their risk, so they tend to be overly conservative with the market value. (I once saw a cartoon that illustrates how each person in the transaction looks at a property in a different way. The seller saw her property as a mansion. The buyer sees it as a shack. The lender saw it the same as the buyer—a shack!)

We were satisfied with the loan that was finally approved. Within our three-day inspection, we also had a contractor out to both properties to confirm our initial rehab estimates. Everything was lined up, and we were prepared to move forward. This meant that we would still have to put up a portion of the closing costs, in this case $2,500 per deal, and the renovation costs we had estimated earlier. These two deals required just over $20,000 of investment, which would have not been possible had I done this myself; I did not have it, and I would have had to go back to my credit cards, and that was not something I wanted to do unless necessary. So even though I gave up 50% of my profit, not only was I going to be able to do the deal, but I was also starting to establish relationships with people who would later help me prosper.

Following my previous retailing plan, I started my marketing process as soon as both homes were painted, cleaned up, and ready to show. Remember, we all need to effectively manage our project time. Having two properties next to one other was an effective use of my time, because I was able to inspect and show both properties at the same time.

Allow me to get back into marketing at this juncture, if I may, as your savvy approach to this can make you rich. I picked up a tip from another investor who taught me how to specifically target local, potential homeowners with clever signs. It also served as a good lesson on how to sell real estate. Allow me to illustrate with an analogy. Most high-end new car buyers want to know exactly how much the purchase price of a car is before they buy. Conversely, most used car buyers don't even know their final sales price until they've signed the loan agreement; they typically spend most of their time negotiating their payment ("What's the monthly?"). So what's this have to do with real estate? My approach to selling homes is similar to that of used car lots; I try to sell payment, not price. Of course the buyer will know the price of the home, but I put all my marketing and all my energy into how much her projected payment will be. So I make a homemade sign that tells prospective buyers the home is for sale, how much down payment is required, and how much the principle, interest, projected property insurance, and property taxes payment/mortgage will be per month. That way, when I get a call from a potential buyer who has seen the sign and likes the home's appearance, she knows all the particulars already—the down payment and the monthly payment—and the potential buyer usually has a good idea if she can afford the home. This, as you can imagine, helps qualify the potential buyer before I say one word to her. So, at a glance, I am able to prequalify people quickly and efficiently. The first wave of calls is very important and needs to be taken seriously, because this first wave is the entire immediate circle of influence (usually within a half or square mile) of a property.

In this instance, and because of my aggressive direct marketing strategy, I was able to find good buyers fairly fast. What's fast? In a matter of weeks! For the two-bedroom, one-bath, I spoke to seven different people. Out of seven, three did not qualify because of credit issues, three never took the initiative to move forward and make a decision, but . . . the last one did qualify, and bingo! I had found my buyer.

I connected my buyer with one of my mortgage brokers. I was asking $130,000 for the two-bedroom, one-bath, and I was offering a 6% seller contribution toward the buyer's closing costs in order to help move the home faster. This buyer was a single mother with two young children. She worked for a security company. When I received her first call, I asked all my qualifying questions right way. Does she rent? How much does she rent for? (How much rent she is paying gives me a very good indication to how much money she can afford per month. If your house would cost the potential buyer $1,500 a month, but she's only paying $500 a month at this point, you need to make sure she can afford triple the monthly overhead. You, as a seller, want to make sure your buyer will be able to afford the monthly payments; the worst thing you can do is not establish that upfront, go for a contract, and bring it all the way to a 30-day closing, only to find the devastating news that this buyer can't afford it.) Oh yes, ask when the buyer wants to move in to the property! These questions will give you a good feel quickly and allow you to qualify the person on the other end.

This particular buyer was not very happy with her current living situation. She had an absentee landlord who was neglecting the property and making their living conditions difficult. I felt pretty comfortable with this buyer since I had my mortgage broker doing the loan, and I offered the buyer the option to move in and rent the home while we did the paperwork to close. Sometimes, that helps solidify the buyer, especially if her current living situation is not ideal. You have to go case-by-case, and I was moving forward diligently to close this deal. So this was a win-win situation, and she was extremely happy that she could improve her financial life and her lifestyle. Once the deal closed, she would already be moved in and then start paying the mortgage instead of rent. A warning: Don't do this if you are not comfortable with the borrower's ability to close the loan. You certainly don't want to be forced into a rental situation when you're looking to sell the property. But giving this buyer the option to move in before closing gave me a good amount of leverage. And that leverage helped when I put the contract price at $130,000. I got no resistance on my asking price; she never even tried to bring me down from my $130,000. We put the property under contract for $130,000 (don't forget I was contributing 6%, or $7,800, so I was really selling at $122,200, still a nice profit), and I was renting the property to her, which would help me with my monthly mortgage payment until it closed.

A couple weeks after my buyer moved in, she called, saying that her plumbing was backed up. I sent a plumber to find out what had happened. He told me that a pipe that goes from the home to the city sewer needed to be changed. Remember, I was still a rookie, and the cost of this job was $1,800. This was a bit shocking to me, but when you are a rookie these things just happen. Instead of getting upset and frustrated, I realized that I can't control what's underground; this was the cost of doing business, and the reason I like to take a percentage for errors and incidentals. This incident helped me grow as an investor by learning to treat it like a business and not get upset, emotional, or discouraged. And to this day I never let these unexpected expenses and sticker shocks bother me because it's part of the business; I tried not to worry about what I can't control.

So I bit the bullet, took care of the sewer line, and pushed for closing. Keep in mind that while you have tenants or potential buyers you need to make sure they're happy, because you are still in the process of selling your property. Your response time is crucial, and management of the property is vital to keeping a healthy business relationship with your clients.

Shortly after that incident, we had our closing, and I made a very nice profit on the property. We had purchased a property for $66,000, put in about $10,000 of renovations, and $5,000 in closing costs. Since we had the property rented, we covered our carrying costs. Even though we sold the property for $130,000, we actually netted $122,200. Deduct $2,500 in closing costs on our end as sellers, and we were left with $119,700. We were into the property for about $81,000. This left an approximate profit of $38,700. Divide that by two, and I had a profit of $19,350: not bad for my third project.

Now let's go back to deal number 2, the three-bedroom, two-bath home. My original thought was to retail this home using the same strategy as the two-bedroom, one-bath home. I placed a sign with the terms specified earlier. Even though my original plan was to retail the home, you never know what kind of buyer will come around. I had a lot of calls because of the sign, but I wasn't finding the right buyer. I tried qualifying a few people, but their credit was not good or they couldn't afford the monthly payments. Keep in mind that as you invest in the blue-collar or lower-income areas, you may have to go through a number of buyers until you find one with good credit. The property renovation took about a month to finish, and though I aggressively marketed the property from the start, I had had no luck to date, unlike the other deal, where it only took me a few weeks to find a buyer. Though the other deal took only a few weeks to put together, things don't always happen the way you want them to. But failure is not an option. All this meant was that I needed to intensify my marketing efforts. So now I had a sign in front of the property, and I was running an ad to try to attract an investor who would want a rental property below market.

The property was worth $150,000. I did my numbers. I was into the property for about $93,000. So I did not sit on the property for too long; I decided to simultaneously continue to pursue a retail buyer and promote this property to investors for $120,000 (in this case, I would not contribute 6% toward the buyer's closing costs). This would net me approximately $27,000 in profit. Still not a bad situation.

What I'm about to say is very important. You must try to stick to my formula. Why? Because if you buy using my criteria, even if you need to blow out the property at a discount, you should still be in a position to make money. You always want to be on the profit side of the equation! You want to say to yourself, "Well, am I going to make $20,000, or am I going to make $15,000, or am I going to make $10,000?" If you take less profit, it's still profit. You want to be in the plus side of this business and not have to take losses in order to unload the property.

This property was not moving at the pace that I had expected it to move. So I ran a new ad in the newspaper and I wrote, "Investor's special! Market value $150,000, will sell $125,000." I was actually willing to take as little as $120,000, but gave myself room for the buyer to negotiate the price down.

I got quite a few calls. I must have spoken to more than 50 people. I qualified many of them by asking the usual questions: "Have you invested like this before? Are you working with a mortgage broker? How are you paying for this property, cash or financing? Are you looking to live there, or are you looking to rent?" (Because even though you're attracting investors, sometimes owner-occupants do call in hopes of getting a good deal on a home.) After taking a lot of calls, I finally found a guy who qualified. He offered me $115,000. I told him that since I was asking $125,000, why didn't we split the $10,000 difference down the middle and meet each other halfway? This worked, and I was under contract to sell the property for $120,000.

Now, dealing with an investor is a bit different from my previous two-bedroom, one-bath example. With the investor, nobody moved in until closing. The investor was a mortgage broker himself. (I can't emphasize enough that mortgage brokers are a very good source of networking. Mortgage brokers work with buyers, and a lot of brokers themselves are investors; and of course, because of their involvement in the business, they understand the mortgage aspect of it.) His being in the business saved time, and we had a fairly quick closing. I sold the property at a discount for $120,000, less $3,000 in closing costs, so I netted $117,000. I was into the property for $93,000, which left me a profit of $24,000. Dividing by two and giving half to my chef/investor meant I personally made $12,000. So, between these two deals I made about $30,000 in profit, and I established myself with a hard money lender—not bad. We also turned these properties over within five months of acquisition. This was impressive, and the next time we went to the hard money lender, our loan amounts were much more generous. Not only did he lend us the full asking price but also the closing costs and some portion of the rehab. Showing results quickly raises your stock as an investor in the eyes of the people who can help you, i.e., the private lenders. This transaction reinforced my decision to walk the uncertain path of real estate rather than the guaranteed path of a job, because in life whenever there are guarantees, there are always limitations. In real estate, there are no guarantees. But at the same time, opportunities are boundless. Here, I'd made this money with no cash out of my pocket. There is a term used in many investment textbooks, including the only real estate class I took in college: OPM, or Other People's Money. When you work smart and deal honestly with people, you can profit, and that "Other Person" who invested with, and in you, will profit right alongside you. Nothing wrong with that!

Here are some lessons from this transaction:

You must develop the ability to visualize potential

Try to work on "seeing" the final product even during your first visit to a property.

Don't try to reinvent the wheel

Just get on it and start rolling. Many people have done what you are attempting to do, and many will after you. Use their experience!

When Selling to Owner Occupied

Focus on a payment, not a price, when selling an "owner-occupied" deal.

Things come up that you will not foresee. You need to be able to stay cool and calm. Continue to focus on what is important—selling.

When involved in property management

You must be able to respond rapidly to any tricky situation that may arise.

Case Study Four

10 Townhomes=Big Profits

Networking, as I have been emphasizing, is an important aspect of real estate investments. Think back to how things worked when you were in school. The students who got together and networked with one another were able to get more done as a group. Similarly, as an individual investor, there is so much real estate to buy and so many ways to buy that it's nearly impossible for one person to cover all the bases. One person can't physically and financially purchase everything. Through networking, you are able to access so much more and do it with a lot less work.

For example, if you want to work pre-foreclosures (contacting homeowners who are in default on their loans but before they lose their properties), it takes lots of money for marketing, lots of physical effort, and a lot of time to exploit this avenue of acquisition—if you want to concentrate in these area, it's fine, but this would have to be your main focus. But if you know an investor already working in this particular field of acquisition and he does all the legwork and finds the right deals, and he's willing to wholesale (make a quick profit), this can leverage your time and money. As long as you can still buy at a good price, networking with this particular individual may prove invaluable. I have purchased a large percentage of my properties from other investors. The next case study will illustrate how profitable leveraging through your network partners can be.

What may surprise you is the number of deals I've done where I bought or sold from another investor like me. You may think that other investors know too much and would only sell something that would be a poor investment. You may think they have a "catch" to every sale. You may believe that no investor will buy from you because you couldn't possibly offer them the kind of great deal they might get from non-pro. Not true!

Other investors face the same challenges that you face: obtaining financing, overcoming marketing hurdles, having the connections and capital to complete complex renovations, and more. Obviously, not all investors will consider wholesaling their properties, but you will be surprised at how many investors will at least entertain the notion of grabbing a quick profit with little effort. This is an area where your reputation and ability to communicate are most crucial, because you are dealing with savvy pros.

There are many ways to find the type of investors you may need. Here are some:

- Join real estate investor clubs.

  There is a constant flow of new people at these venues. Everyone in attendance has a motivation and a desire to get involved. It's usually very easy to strike up conversations with people in this environment.

- Attend courthouse tax deed sales and meet people there.

  Most people who attend these sales are investors. The complexity of these types of sales and the cash requirement tend to eliminate most homeowners.

- Advertise in the newspapers for properties that are obviously being sold by investors (just like I did with my first deal).

  If you spend time looking at the classified ads, you will learn to spot ads written by other investors. Investors' ads use more attention-getting words, such as "Handyman," "Must sell," "Bank-owned," "Needs work," "Make offers."

- Examine the tax records and look for company names of investors or individuals who are, again and again, buying and selling.

  When you check the tax records and search sales comparisons, you can find names of both sellers and buyers. Look for a trend. If you see the same buyer buying and selling, he or she may be someone you want to contact for good networking connections. I've had other investors and Realtors contract me on a regular basis because they see me or my companies constantly pop up on tax records.

- Have you seen signs in your neighborhood that read "I buy properties for cash?" Call them.

This is someone letting the world know he is involved in the business, so why not phone him?

- Foreclosure sale proceedings—most people attending will be investors, not wanna-be homeowners. Similar to the tax deed sale approach.
- Cold-call probate and estate attorneys; offer to buy them lunch, because they will see a steady stream of properties for sale. It's their business. (Professionals who represent estates are also a great source.)

This next deal has proved to be very profitable. I got a call one afternoon from a contact who had been working quite a long time with a partner. Really nice guys. I had met them at a local area investor get-together. (I have previously mentioned how important it is to be a good salesperson when you get involved in real estate. It's also important to be successful at selling yourself. The more people trust you, like you, and enjoy dealing with you, the more opportunities will arise. You must constantly work on your people skills and your communication skills. This is a people business, right? Your ability to relate to others is beyond valuation. That is why I am driving this point home again and again!)

The sellers told me that they had a contract with a bank to purchase a project. The closing was only 30 days off. The investment consisted of 10 townhomes, with identical three-bedroom, two-and-a-half-bath, and two-story floor plans. All were a part of their own small subdivision. The seller gave me the address and told me that that each would be the same price. They were asking $72,000 per townhome.

I took down the information and asked how much work I would need to put into them. They told me some needed more work than others. They also told me I would have 28 days to close. I got on the computer, pulled up the address through the tax roll, and found that the owner was a bank. Which means the bank had foreclosed on the property and now was selling it. I did a few comparable market analyses to see what had sold in the area. I was valuing 10 separate townhomes, but the only sales in the area were single-family homes—not necessarily identical structures for establishing market value. The single-family homes ranged from $155,000 to $200,000. I felt that I needed some help to establish the true market value. As good as you may get in different aspects of this business, sometimes you need help. It may be a renovation that is over your head, and you cannot come up with a cost without professional help. Or, as in this case, you may need assistance in establishing a concrete market value. The bottom line is, if you feel you need help, you probably do. You need to listen to your gut instinct.

My Rolodex really came into play in this example. I discussed having a variety of title companies, appraisers, contractors, attorneys, and so forth at my disposal. I dipped into this and called a trusted appraiser. I explained that I was looking at these townhomes, but the only comps I could find in the area were single-family homes, which, of course, were not the apples-to-apples comparison necessary. I asked what he thought the market value might be if he were doing the appraisal. His answer could save a tremendous investment of my time. I realized that single-family homes were more readily marketable than units that share common walls, and without a solid price "comp," I could not take this on. The appraiser told me he'd get back to me after pursuing some research.

The next day, the appraiser gave me a call back and told me that he had made some adjustments to the single-family comps, and he believed that each townhome was valued at $140,000. Well, this was great news. I immediately called the investors and made sure the property was still available. I didn't want to drive there and do a lot of physical research only to find out the property was no longer available. Luckily, the townhomes were still available. I drove to the property, and I noticed it was on a major street with a lot of exposure. Across the street stood brand-new apartments built by a developer as a rental community. To get a feel for the competition, I called the rental office to find out what kinds of units were available and what they were asking for rents. They had both two- and three-bedroom units for rent, and they were going for $1,200 to $1,500. That was also great news for my potential new investment. As I drove to the townhomes, I noticed that all 10 were set together in a little mini-cluster. Apparently, in the past there had had a homeowners association, now dissolved.

So this particular project consisted of 10 attractive townhomes not connected to any other property. They were all vacant. As I walked through the properties, I noticed each had central A/C, though some units needed replacing. They all required carpet and tile, some of them needed new kitchens, and a few needed new roofs. I made notes on each individual unit and how much each one would need in work. Another good point was all 10 were right next to each other, so management would be much easier than having 10 units in 10 different locations. This would make the deal not only attractive to me but also to potential lenders, since they would understand that this project could be efficiently managed. I concluded that each unit needed $7,000 in renovation.

I crunched the numbers. I believed the properties were worth $140,000 and required a $7,000-per-unit renovation investment. Therefore, 70% of market value ($140,000) gave me $98,000, and then deducting $7,000 for renovations and $13,000 for the closing costs and holding time gave me a final number of $78,000, and that would be the most I was willing to pay. They were asking $72,000, which put this clearly within my range.

Back in my office, I prepared a contract and then called the investors to let them know I'd be sending it over. They informed me that they now had multiple offers, and they would need my highest and best offer. This was unfortunate, and what I had hoped to avoid. Nonetheless, I worked as fast as I could, knowing this was a good deal. It would not last long, and I was likely competing with people who would be just as reliable as I. Remember: If you find a good deal, you need to move as fast as you can! I remember thinking that the extra day it had taken for the appraiser to get back to me may have cost me the deal. But, understanding the true market value is critical, and you need to take the time or risk serious trouble. If you lose a deal in the process, well, it just was not meant to be.

When there is a multiple-offer situation, and this is pretty common in a competitive market, you just need to put your best offer on the table and hope for the best. Since I was able to pay up to $78,000 and they were asking $72,000, I had to make the strongest offer I could. Remember, I really liked the large, three-bedroom, two-and-a-half bath floor plans, and having them all next to each other injected a lot of marketability to it. So I made a full offer of $78,000 per unit and faxed my offer to the seller.

The next day, I received a call informing me that I had the best offer. Not the highest offer, but the best offer. What do I mean by that?

The terms of the contract are sometimes as important as the price itself. Another buyer offered $81,000 per townhome, but he was using conventional financing, and the contract was subject to financing. I was using private financing. The red tape that comes with conventional financing could have delayed the closing. The sellers had less than four weeks to close. They couldn't chance being put in a tight spot. So, naturally, the seller preferred a stronger offer with no contingencies on financing or inspections from a buyer who would move rapidly. That offer was mine. Making offers and being able to come through under tight circumstances makes you a stronger buyer who may often get a lower price than a more traditional opponent. It's very important to understand that.

I was excited! I must say this project was very invigorating for me even though it would mean a lot of work; it also had the potential to reward my efforts with strong profits. I had a really good spread on each townhome, and the profits were times 10.

The next step: secure my financing. At this point, understanding the criteria of the lenders you're working with makes the lending process much easier. Since the property had many attractive attributes, I felt pretty comfortable that I wouldn't have to work hard to find my loans. The lender didn't like that I was requesting a larger than normal cash-out over my purchase price, due to this being a 10-unit deal. I was asking for 70% of the market value of $140,000, times 10, which after closing costs would amount to about $100,000 that I would get when I purchase the property. Remember, I was buying all 10 townhomes at once, so my loan request was higher than my purchase price; being that it was 10-fold, it translated to a larger cash-out at the time of acquisition. Keep in mind that transactions like this do occur, but they're not common. To pull it off, you need to have bring a very strong deal to a lender with whom you enjoy a solid and trusting relationship.

The lender suggested that we put any excess money needed for renovations into an escrow account and release it as the work was completed, similar to a draw. And that's the way he was comfortable lending the money. It's not an unusual request, and something that is often done with private and hard money lenders. In most cases, when you borrow more than the cost of the property, the lenders put that extra money into escrow so the money is not just pocketed by careless investors. I had no issues with this request. In fact, I was thrilled that this was the only issue that the lender raised.

As always, even when you find a great deal and secure the necessary financing, you still have to make sure that the title is good and that there aren't any major liens or violations. That's what a title company is for. Such issues could prevent you from receiving good title and being able to actually purchase the property. As we got close to closing, the title company's searches from the county were coming in, and we found out a few violations still existed on the property. (Remember: Once a property goes to foreclosure, all the liens and monetary fees are foreclosed and wiped out, but the violations still exist.)

Since I was going to improve the properties, most of the violations were part of the work I was going to do anyway and weren't something that would kill the project. In this particular case, three roofs needed to be redone and required an inspection from the city. Another violation came in for improper electrical wiring. We had not planned to hire a licensed electrician. Since buyers are able to review the title search before closing, I was able to get estimates from a licensed electrician. This required an extra few thousand dollars over our original estimate. This was not damaging enough to walk away from the deal. I chose to move forward and deal with the violations situation once I owned the property. Finally, it was closing day, and all went as I had hoped.

We started by renovating one unit at a time. Of course,

foremost in our thoughts was our selling strategy. I decided to market the properties as rentals right away, since having 10 units vacant would brutalize our monthly cash flow. I did not know what kind of buyers I would find, and focused on renovating and renting the units as soon as possible. As soon as a unit was completed, I took action to get it rented. I ran an ad in the paper. Having the property on a major street helped me with rent sign exposure. I listed the townhomes for rent for $1,100 each and since my mortgage was $900, I was definitely not losing money each month. This meant I would not have to unduly rush but could seek a buyer willing to pay what I wanted. I did not want to be forced into a "fire sale" in order to stop any bleeding of cash flow.

I also put the properties on the list in the local Section 8 office. Section 8 is a federal- and state-sponsored program for low-income housing. The government assists the tenant with his or her monthly rent. As a landlord, you need to pass a move-in inspection and then an annual inspection thereafter in order to maintain these programs. The demand was strong. I did not have a problem finding tenants. The location was good, the units spacious and freshly remodeled. Within three months of closing on the property, I had filled all the units with tenants. Of course, being a landlord comes with some headaches.

Since I was in such a hurry to fill the units up, I had given a couple of tenants favorable move-in terms. In other words, instead of charging first, last, and security, I charged first and security, meaning tenants needed less than the usual amount to get moved in. I learned the hard way that this may get you tenants who are unable to pay on time. I started to experience late payments, and finally non-payments. Sometimes (as I had to learn the hard way, but you can learn from my mistakes) you are so eager to get people into a rental that you tend not to properly screen them, do background checks, get references, or get proper move-in money. In my situation, here I was making my mortgage payment and spending money for attorneys and court costs. This experience has certainly helped me understand the importance of proper management and screening.

Meanwhile, I placed my property in the multiple-listing service. Even though the project was composed of 10 separate townhomes, it could prove attractive to a "buy, hold, and rent" investor. I received myriad calls, but found few serious buyers willing to make the move. As it turned out, the sellers of my townhomes, of all people, contacted me with a lead. They often came across buyers for whom they had no properties that fit the bill. They looked at sending referrals to me as a way to pick up a few bucks here and there.

So, my townhome sellers referred me to an investor who wanted to purchase rental properties. The marketability and close proximity of my units made them an excellent choice. The investor was a female police officer. It seems to me law enforcement is actually a good job to have as a landlord; it provides you with a lot of presence and often the flexible hours that an investor requires.

She wanted to buy five townhomes and perhaps the other five somewhere down the road. Since I was not in a hurry and I was covering my mortgage, I went ahead and put five under contract. I was asking $129,900 per townhome. We negotiated the sales price to $127,500 each. I offered $2,500 per unit as a finder's fee to the investor who had referred me to the buyer, netting me $125,000 per unit. But $125,000 was my rock-bottom minimum, so I required that she pay all closing costs, including what is customarily paid by the seller; I would not accept $125,000 less $2,000 or so in closing costs.

We signed the contract. The buyer had her own mortgage broker. The closing took quite a while. We initially had 45 days to close, but the buyer was taking longer to get the job done. Since we'd been communicating and working on closing it together and the properties were rented, I gave the buyer extensions for additional deposits. Nearly 80 days after we had signed the contract, the closing was complete.

I sold five of the 10 townhomes and made a cool $125,000 profit. And the best news was I was only halfway done. Still, three months after continually marketing the townhomes, I'd yet to find another buyer willing to take all five. So I decided to contact the woman who had purchased the first five to see if I could entice her to take the whole shebang. It made all the sense in the world for her to take the other five. She would need time if she were to get this deal done, but sometimes you need to be patient in order to hold onto a good buyer. Sometimes if you're too eager and you seem pushy and desperate, buyers get turned off and stay away from your deal.

So I was patient. I had already made a good amount of money, and the properties were rented and paying for themselves.

But my intention was still to sell these townhomes. So I told my previous buyer that I would sell her the other five for a discount if she could commit soon. I offered her the property for $122,500. She felt it was a good opportunity, and she decided to buy the other five townhomes.

It was a delicate balancing act. You see, if I had tried to push her too soon I would have lost her. She was an inexperienced investor and still felt a bit overwhelmed by the first five townhomes. Luckily, I had made sure I followed up with her on a regular basis, even after the sale. I wanted to demonstrate that I would see her through the deal and assist her with her property management tasks. You see, if you are attempting to establish yourself in this business and you are trying to develop a good track record and referral base, you need to follow up with your buyers. Since she was new and taking on rental properties, I told her I was more than happy to help and only a phone call away. If she was satisfied with the deal, she might buy more from me later, and since we already had a relationship, it would be much easier the next time around. I always tell my buyers, regardless of whether they are investors or home owners, if I treat you right and do well by you, you will come back to me or send me a referral. It just makes good business sense. So I had to give her time to get her feet wet before moving into deeper waters, yet still inch her forward. As it turned out, the buyer used the same mortgage broker she had used for the original five townhomes. About 60 days later, I had my second batch of five townhomes sold.

Being a good networking investor, I honored my referral fee to the original investor who had sent her to me. I did not have to do it. But displaying honesty and going the extra mile have helped me stay successful in a competitive business.

Since I was getting a bit less per unit, I gave him $1,500 for each townhome. It still came out to $7,500 for doing no additional work. But don't forget, without his referral I would not have found my buyer to begin with, so it really wasn't for nothing. As for me, I collected an additional profit of $100,000. Within one year, I made a profit of $225,000 on this one project alone. The power of networking with investors—not only to buy but also to sell properties—has proved to be invaluable in my real estate career, as it will in yours.

Here are some lessons from this transaction:

Other investors go though the same challenges as you do

So don't feel that they won't want to flip the property to you. Try! You may be surprised at the results.

Your ability to relate to others is vital

Selling yourself and the ability to be trusted is something that you need to work on all the time.

Sometimes, knowing what you don't know is also important. Be humble

Try to ask for help from professionals when you are not sure; this is important. This will almost always keep you out of trouble.

Have integrity and take care of people who can help you

If you are here for the long run, this is a must.

Look to a management company for help when called for in order to avoid landlord pitfalls.

Case Study Five

Quiet Title Challenge

As you'll soon see, this next deal was fraught with challenges. But with the challenges came a wonderful lesson: as long as you buy a property right (meaning the right price) and manage it right (with care and diligence), you should always stay out of the red (not lose money!).

As I was proceeding through my usual "looking for properties" routine one day, I ran into an investor-targeted ad in the local paper. The ad trumpeted, "Handyman property. Four-bedroom, two-bath home for sale." I called.

The seller, as I had suspected, happened to be another investor. He seemed like a decent guy, and he had some apparent experience. I knew he understood the business and would be easy to work with. What do I mean easy to work with? Many private sellers or new investors let personal considerations get in the way; if you make a low offer, they may get insulted because, in their minds, they live in the finest home in the land. Or, their lack of knowledge may mean that they are unable to adjust or improvise or accept changes in terms. Pros learn that the most important thing is getting the deal done and making some kind of profit; they learn the ideal is seldom reachable, and they are willing to compromise accordingly and keep their emotions out of it. Amateurs can become entrenched and may stubbornly refuse to accept any changes, even if it means killing a deal. These people may just dig in their heels for the wrong reasons.

As I proceeded to find out more about this deal, I asked him if he owned the property. I was trying to find out if he was trying to wholesale this property, which would mean he may have a deadline to close. I would have to live by his deadline. Being a possible new buyer, you want to know what the terms the seller is dealing with because they definitely affect you. As it turned out, he owned it already. Through questioning (be pushy to find out as much as you can—it will save you TIME), I found out that he had purchased the property through a tax deed sale at the local courthouse. Then I asked a bit about the property itself: he told me the roof needed work, some cosmetics were rough, and it had a shed that needed to be demolished per city orders. (I listened to him, even though I always do my own due diligence later.) He was asking $105,000. I got on the computer and started my research on the property through the tax roll record. And here is the actual tax roll (record) and what is most important to study:

Above is the info that I consider most vital. The format may vary from town to town depending on the software you use. But looking at the tax roll above (not the comps), the numbers in bold are the important things to study. I noticed, when I analyzed the property, that the seller's name (which gives me an idea who the seller purchased the property from) was the county. The deed type was a tax deed, and the seller was the Clerk of Circuit Court. So this confirmed that the seller had purchased this property through the county via a tax deed sale.

As discussed earlier, tax deeds have positive and negative issues. It's great that you can get a really good deal, but as you know, in life many bargains come with strings attached. As a real estate investor, you need to make sure that you're buying a property with as clean a title as possible. You're investing a great deal of time and money, and you certainly don't want to have a problem with legalities. When you buy a tax deed from the county, you must pay cash the same day of your winning bid. In exchange, the city provides you with a deed. That deed does not ensure against any problems with title, or against any violations, liens, or any encumbrances on the property. Unlike buying a property in a conventional manner (going through a title policy, getting a mortgage, and making sure you get title insurance), tax deeds are anything but conventional. This means the investor must do careful research before purchasing the property. Further, once you purchase the property, you must take any necessary steps to gain clear title. Therefore, once you purchase a tax deed, you must begin a process called "quiet title." Quiet title is similar to the foreclosure process. A quiet title process goes through the courts and makes sure that nobody out there can come back and claim interest on the property you just purchased. Before any title company can issue title insurance (which will guarantee and secure your investment from anybody claiming rights to your property), you must hire an attorney and have him complete the steps required for the quiet title procedure. This can take anywhere from three months to a year.

I also noticed that the seller was marketing this house as a single-family home, but the zoning was for a duplex. Knowing that, I spoke to the seller and asked if the property had already gone through this quiet title procedure. The seller informed me that it had. Before looking at the property physically, I looked at the square footage and number of beds and baths (which is not always as accurate when looking at the tax roll, because that information is only as good as the person who entered it), lot size, year built, and tax-assessed value. Then I looked at the sales to see what had sold in the area. Based on my research above, the property was worth $185,000; 70% of $185,000 is $129,500. Though I'd not yet seen the property, based upon my conversation with the seller, I estimated the renovation at $15,000. Subtracting $15,000 from my base purchase maximum of $129,500 gave me $114,500. Finally, from that number I deducted $12,000 for the cost of holding and closing the property, which left me with the base purchase price of $102,500. The seller, as you recall, was asking $105,000. I offered $100,000 with a three-day inspection period, and the seller accepted. The seller faxed me over a contract with the usual seller-biased terms on the contract. In the meantime, I drove to the property and made sure my initial $15,000 assessment of the renovation was on target.

As I drove in, I noticed that the neighborhood appeared a little rundown. What do I mean? A number of people were just sort of hanging around on the sidewalks at a time when most of us would be working. This may indicate a lower unemployment rate for the area. Here and there, I found boarded-up, abandoned homes. Many real estate investor signs had sprouted up in the yards; signs, in many ways, meant this was an active investor area. Even with a neighborhood such as this, as long as I could get a really good price I knew I'd be able to profit.

Once at the home, I found wire mesh in front, half of it fallen down and curled up on the ground. I liked the attached carport. I could see that it would need paint and a new roof and that the fence would have to be repaired.

I had to keep in mind while walking through that the property was zoned as a duplex. Always remember when you buy a house that you're buying all the quirky modifications made by past owners over the years. As an investor, you need to determine what the original floor plan was, the original structure of the home, and if any manipulation to the original floor plan or structure has been undertaken.

Knowing that the house was a duplex and now being marketed as a single-family home, I had to be cautious about what I was inheriting. It was apparent that this was originally a duplex, but previous owners must have broken through a few walls and combined the original pair of two-bedroom, one-bath units into a four-bedroom, two-bath, single-family home. Luckily for me, it had been done well.

I kept in mind that if I wished to bring this back to its original duplex design, either by my choice or because the city forced me to do so, my costs would be greater than if I renovated it in its present single-family home configuration.

The current modifications were acceptable so long as they were legal from the city's point of view. If the modifications were not done with the proper permits or completed to code, any changes, again, had to be economically viable.

This particular home had been set up as a four-bedroom, two-bath home now for many years. The home needed a new roof, new flooring, and new kitchen, and the bathrooms had to be brought up to date. My guess on the renovation of $15,000 might have been somewhat high, and after looking at the house, I thought the home needed closer to $12,000, but I kept it at $15,000, for a rainy day. I learned, after calling the city and inquiring about the property, that the changes that had been made to the floor plan (from duplex to single) were "grandfathered," and so could be retained. I called the city to find out how many beds and baths they had officially listed. They confirmed four bedrooms and two baths. The title company would later do a full title search, as well as searches for any liens or violations.

After looking at the market value, renovation costs, and price, I decided to put the property under contract. Everything seemed to be lined up, and then it was time to move forward toward acquisition.

I waived my three-day inspection period, handed over the $1,000 deposit, executed the contract in full, and waited to close. Wait a minute! Why would I waive the three-day inspection? Being a full-time investor, the quicker I get the deal under way, the closer I get to a profit.

I started working on my financing. I contacted the same three lenders I preferred to work with. Based on the $185,000 market value, I requested a loan of $125,000. Based on the purchase price, the market value, and my relationship with the lenders, attaining that loan amount should not have been difficult. As an investor and what I call a "conductor" of the investment process, you are constantly performing multiple tasks. For example, here I was working with the lender and also working with a title company toward closing. And everyone would keep me jumping.

A week before closing, my title company telephoned and gave me two different issues that were bad news. The first, the more serious of the two, was that the attorney who had performed the previous quiet title action had done it improperly, leaving a few necessary steps undone. The second was that there were physical violations that needed to be taken care of. There was a shed that needed to be removed in the back of the property. Also, the rundown fence in the front needed to be removed. Both of the physical violations were no big deal, since I was planning on doing that as part of my renovation anyway; with a good plan and proper execution, it also could be handled.

But—the attorney's botched job rendered the property title uninsurable. Knowing this, 99% of the lenders would not lend. Title insurance is vital to protect the lender's position as well as the buyers. When a lender invests money in a property in the form of a loan, the lender's security consists of the borrower's personal guarantee of the note, property insurance (in case anything physically happens to the property), and title insurance (in case anyone else claims rights to the property). So, not being able to buy title insurance put me in a pickle. The stronger your relationship with private lenders and the more faith they have in your ability as an investor, the more they will be willing to pursue the process and continue with a loan. Keep in mind that as an investor you can find a good deal, you can negotiate the price, you can put the property under contract and even have it sold to another buyer, but if something mucks up the title, you may not be able to actually purchase the property. All this is out of your direct control, and it can prevent the completion of a deal. At any rate, you don't want to buy a property that will present a problem passing clear title.

What did I do? Remember, in real estate everything has a price. So instead of walking away from a good deal (which is what most people do), I contacted a quiet title attorney who specialized in these procedures and asked how long it would take me to get title insurance. As an investor, you must think creatively and do what most people are not willing to do. In this example, I had to solve my seller's problem or renegotiate my position in order to move forward to purchase. The attorney informed me that it would take about three months and $3,000 in order to complete the quiet title procedure. Then I could acquire title insurance. And I learned that just because the seller told me his attorney had handled the quiet title action did not mean it was done right. Not all lawyers are created equal. Just like any professional, some don't do the job correctly.

So I spoke to the seller and told him it would cost me $3,000 to finish the quiet title process and another $3,000 in holding time for my mortgage, taxes, and insurance during this down time. Since I was dealing with an investor who was sympathetic and wanted to sell his property, I figured out a way for both of us to be happy. So we renegotiated the asking price from $100,000 to $94,000.

Another challenge remained: I had to convince the lender to close and lend on this property without title insurance! At this point, my hard money lender and I had a solid bond. I had done quite a bit of business with him, and I explained the situation, informing him that our lawyer would get to work immediately and swiftly to secure title as soon as possible. Luckily enough for me, the lender accepted, and we had a closing.

Once I officially became the property owner, I began marketing and renovating. I also had my lawyer work on the title procedure. The property needed a new roof; that is the first thing you want to do. You don't want a leaky roof to do damage to any work done to the interior.

The only violations that existed when I purchased this property were a shed in the back that needed to be demolished and a fence on the side that needed to be removed. I prepared to pull the necessary permits and close out that case. Just remember, as an investor and a new property owner, you are responsible for the property, for all the good and bad that come with it. Regardless of what happened in the past, whatever history the property has, in the eyes of city officials you are assuming everything. There is no insurance for any current violations, liens, and or infractions. Turns out, what happened next with the city took this investment to a different strategy.

I pulled the permit for the shed, fence, and the roof. My contractor also should have pulled general repair permits for the interior work (you'll recall I was doing cosmetic work throughout), but he did not. When the inspectors came to inspect the fence, shed, and roof, they noticed that I had not pulled permits for the interior work. So I was slapped with fines for doing work to the original structure without proper permits. Now I had to go back and pull permits for every little job I was doing. This required more time, more money, and more hassle. Unfortunately, this was not something I could negotiate. Investors depend on contractors to do their jobs properly, and if they don't, the responsibility falls on the investor.

So I rolled up my sleeves, met with my contractor, and mapped out a timeline of what needed to be done. Instead of the job costing me $15,000, it cost me $17,000 and an extra two months, which cost me about $2,500 in additional mortgage carry. Meanwhile, I marketed this property both for sale and for rent.

The reason I marketed for renting at the same time as selling is because I knew that I was going to sell this particular property to another investor who would most likely want to rent the property anyway. Therefore, having a tenant could help pay the mortgage while

I tried to find the right buyer, and it might be a plus for the new buyer. Soon, I found a tenant. Normally I like to get first, last, and security. I was asking $900 a month and trying to collect $2,700 for the move in. The tenant only had $1,800, but I made a decision to go ahead with just first and security rather than first, last, and security. I wanted someone paying rent and helping to cover my cost of carry! I wrote the lease on a month-to-month basis. That would allow me and a potential future buyer an option to give a tenant a 30-day notice to move out.

I soon found a buyer/investor who wanted to do exactly what I was proposing: he wanted to purchase the property and rent it out. Keep in mind, the property was worth $185,000, and I was selling it for $145,000. I was sticking to my plan of finding a buyer and closing fast for a quick turnover.

This particular buyer was somebody I had met through previous newspaper ads that I had run. Don't forget: for each ad that you run, keep the name and phone number and information on every person who calls you. You can always call them back. You'll be surprised to find that 95% of the time they are still in the business and looking for good deals. So before I try running an ad on any new property I run another ad only after I exhaust the older leads. You'll be amazed at the advantages of staying organized and keeping good records. You'll be able to take maximum advantage of even one small classified ad.

Of course, you now realize how important it is to have a great mortgage broker. The new buyer had his own mortgage broker. Not knowing the mortgage broker, I was a little reluctant, but the buyer was adamant about using his mortgage broker, leaving me with little choice in the matter. We negotiated the price of the home to $142,000, and his mortgage broker would handle the loan. At the same time, the buyer wanted me to give the tenant notice to move out. The buyer wanted to convert the single-family home back into a duplex, which made more sense for the buyer from a cash flow perspective, as the buyer would be in a position to collect two rent checks rather than one.

In the state of Florida, when a tenant is on a month-to-month basis, you need to give him or her 15-day notice to move out.(Check your state's requirements.) So per the buyer's requests I went ahead and prepared a 15-day notice and mailed it to the tenant. The tenant was not happy, but he knew that not obeying the time frame would lead to an eviction. That was not something he or I wanted to go through. I called around to investors and asked them if they had anything to rent in the same area where I had this property. One of the investors did have a nice three-bedroom, one-bath home for rent. I connected my current tenant with this investor friend of mine, and we had a match. Not only did this help me make a smooth transition, but I also looked very good in both the eyes of the tenant and the investor. Two and a half weeks after the notice, the tenant moved out.

Networking with other investors was a good thing in this case because it helped me in making a smooth transition. That was a positive for me in moving the tenant fast, without any complications, and giving the new investor a new tenant. Sometimes you need to think to move ahead and not only try to solve your problems; you also need to try to help the other person deal with his problem as well.

So the tenant moved, and there were about two weeks left before the buyer had to close on the property. During one of my routine follow-up calls with the mortgage broker, I found out that the buyer had some credit complications. During the loan application, the buyer got behind on a couple of his credit card bills. The bank usually pulls the credit in the beginning of the loan application; occasionally, the bank pulls it again toward the end for quality control. Here, the buyer's credit score dropped significantly due to the deficiencies. Consequently, to complete the loan, the bank lowered the total amount it was willing to lend to my buyer. The sales price was $142,000, and the borrower was borrowing 90%, or $127,800. But since the buyer's credit score went down, the bank was only willing to lend him 85% of $142,000 or $120,700, a difference of $7,100 that the buyer would have to come up with. Not surprisingly, the buyer did not have the extra funds to invest. The deal did not close, and the buyer walked away from his $1,000 deposit. So now not only had I jettisoned my tenant, I did not have a buyer! Not a good situation, but definitely a learning experience transaction. I realized I should never have given the tenant notice to move out. I should have waited to close and then let the new buyer give notice and deal with the transition.

So now it was back to the drawing board with more losses due to delays. Now my main focus was to get rid of this property, make the most I could, and move on. I called some of my previous buyers and told them I had a property that I wanted to move at a fantastic price.

That usually helps promote a property, and people think they may get a better deal than normal. I was still asking $145,000, but I was willing to be a bit more flexible. I received an offer of $135,000, and we negotiated to $138,000 with one condition: that the buyer use the mortgage broker I worked with. Since I had lost all that time, I did not want to take any more chances and not have something go through due to a mortgage process. Thirty-five days into the contract, we had a closing, and I sold the property for $135,000. I made a profit of $10,000. That is usually the minimum that I would like to make on a deal that I get involved in. Even though I made some mistakes and cost myself a bit of money, I still consider it a fine learning experience. What is better than learning and making money in the process?

Here are some lessons from this transaction:

When you are talking to potential sellers, ask questions

Get a feel for the deal. I like to know where they got the property from. Are they investors? Homeowners? Flippers? It helps me position my tone and negotiation tactics.

Remember, when buying property, you are inheriting everything that anyone before you has done to the property. Be careful and do your homework. It's not necessarily all bad, as long as you know what you are getting involved in.

Learn to be a problem solver

Not only for your issues, but for anyone around you who can ultimately affect you.

Keep good records when you run ads

This way you will maximize your return on advertising.

Case Study Six

The Single Family Home That Turned into a Duplex

I met a real estate broker at one of the monthly real estate investor networking meetings. We had good chemistry right off the bat; nothing can guarantee a long-term relationship with someone, but a positive first impression is a nice start. This led to a deal that I found particularly interesting, because it brought with it some surprises—some good, some bad. As I mentioned previously, always stay in touch with people who are a good source of leads.

Sticking to this game plan, I'd maintained an ongoing relationship with this agent. He had given me leads in the past, but none had panned out. Sometimes good timing and a little bit of luck help, but not unless you are both consistent and persistent. If I don't diligently follow up and stay in touch with potential sellers, I will miss many opportunities. In fact, the harder I work, the luckier I get. (Here is a quote I keep over my desk in my office: "What is luck? It is nothing more than the marriage of preparation with opportunity.")

I took a call one Wednesday evening about a potential property. The real estate broker gave me the address. I then pulled up the tax roll and examined the following details:

1. The square footage (this gives me an approximate size, which I verify myself when I inspect the property)

2. The address (I need to confirm the address given to me verbally; also, some homes have a different address for mail than they do on the tax roll)

3. The bed and bath count (the tax roll is the official count of beds and baths, but this always needs physical verification), year built (a comparison item that must be used when doing your "comps"; remember, keep your comps to homes of similar year construction)

4. Construction type (the foundation type, the structure of the home—brick or frame, for instance)

5. Lot size (again, the official lot size is here on the tax roll; in the long run, the size of the lot may help or hurt your chance of sale)

6. The current owner (I want to know if I'm dealing with a private owner, bank, or corporation, because who I'm dealing with constitutes a big part of my strategy)

7. When the last purchase of this property was and for what price (sometimes a property may have sold some years ago at much more than I might pay for it now, and that always makes me feel I am on track)

8. The tax-assessed value (very important, as this is the value the county places on a property, and you will pay tax based upon this number; typically, the assessed value is about 30% below market value)

9. The zoning of the property (a big issue; if this is zoned single-family home and you find a duplex there, you may have some legal issues)

These were some pieces of the puzzle that would help me get a feel for what I was looking at.

Once I understand the subject property, it makes it easier to be able to look at the comparable sales and make sure I am comparing apples to apples. Before I physically view a property, I do all the research I can on paper (meaning looking at the tax roll comps and making sure the property makes sense based on the numbers).

Once I determine what the market value is, I compare it

to the price the seller is asking and do a quick analysis to make sure that the asking price is in the ballpark. For example, if the market value is $100,000 and the seller is asking $90,000, I will never go and physically look at this property. If I can only pay, let's say, $60,000 for this property, I would perhaps make a verbal offer or send a letter of intent just to feel out the seller and how flexible he or she is. As an investor, getting in your car and driving to the property costs time and money. If I determine that the property is worth $100,000 and the most I am willing to pay is $55,000, the seller and I are not that far apart if he or she is asking $65,000. Perhaps the seller may demonstrate some flexibility, or after physically looking at the property myself, I may want to increase or even decrease my offer depending on how much I liked the property once I see it.

Back to my deal: Remember, I looked at the comps from the tax roll. How did I get my hands on the tax roll? Good question. The Internet now plays a key role in the access to public information. Depending on the market you're in, there are companies that give you access to online services: public records such as sales, comps, and specific property info—even aerial maps! I subscribed to these services as soon as I knew I wanted to be an investor. Early on in my career when money was an issue, I still subscribed to these services even though they can be a bit pricey. Having the right information to help you make a good and calculated decision is invaluable.

I logged on to this service and custom-fit my search to find closed sales—in this particular situation, I went back six months, for everything in a half-mile radius, and with a similar size of lot and home. The search results give me the:

Sale Price

Living Area

Price per Sq Ft

Year Built

Lot Size

Bedroom Count

Bathroom count

Number of Stories

Total Value

All of this not only on my subject property, but on my area comps; it also displays the high, low, and average of each of these numbers! This is similar to the Internet-based service that many banks and appraisers use to come to decisions about the same property. Let me mention how important it is to use the same information source as everyone else involved in the sale. It will simplify your life and ensure continuity.

Based on the square footage, year built, and lot size, I determined the property to be worth $150,000.

The bank, through the agent, was asking $95,000. This was a property worth looking at.

The following morning, I got into my car and headed to the property. Shortly after I arrived, I found out that this was a corner property that had definitely been neglected for a substantial amount of time. The grass and weeds were extremely high, and the property showed signs of vandalism. Window glass was broken, the front door consisted of a big piece of plywood that was nailed to the wall, and the exterior paint was badly chipped. This would normally scare off the average buyer, but as an investor and someone who was trying to get a good deal, this was exactly what I was looking for. The property also had a fence all around the structure. I made my way around the property and started to look around with my "contractor" hat on. Since the front door was covered with a sheet of plywood for security reasons, I went to the back door. With the lockbox combination that the Realtor had given to me, I found the key to open the back door. I always carry a flashlight because most properties that are distressed do not have electricity or even running water. (In the past, I have mentioned using professional inspectors. Most professional property inspectors will not inspect a property that does not have running utilities; you need to find inspectors or contractors who will work under these conditions.) Contractors/handymen are a better choice, since the inspection will lead to a job for them.

So I entered through the back door of the property first. When I walk through a house for the first time, I like to have a piece of paper and a pen to take notes on the property. I also filled out the property inspection analysis sheet. I use the printout of the tax roll of the actual property I am evaluating for my notes. That way, if I do not purchase this property or somebody else beats me to it, I file my research for a back-up offer. If the highest bidder for this property does not come through, I can retrieve my tax roll comps and comments on the renovations. (In many cases, of course, the seller accepts a higher offer. That doesn't mean that the highest offer will actually close; it means that somebody else has a contract to purchase this property. You don't want to throw away all the research you did, because if the highest bidder does not buy the property, the seller will look at the other offers that were made and try to sell it to them. I have purchased quite a number of properties after someone else has over-bid me but could not ultimately close.)

Making my way through the property, I noticed the kitchen cabinets were badly deteriorated. The kitchen had to be completely redone: the bathroom needed a new toilet, vanity and fixtures, tub, and tile throughout. The property needed to be painted, inside and outside, new tile flooring throughout, and a complete clean-up.

I estimated the renovation would cost $11,500. Back at my office, I re-analyzed the property; having seen it physically, I could combine that information with my paper evaluation and truly determine what the property was worth in market condition. When I studied the tax roll, I noticed that the property was zoned as a duplex, yet I had only seen one structure with a fence around it. Curious . . .

In this particular neighborhood, the houses were built in the 1950s, and a lot can happen to structures in half a century. Often, neighborhoods have a combination of single-family homes and multi-family homes, so even though this property was zoned multi-family, it could still have been just a single-family home.

After looking at the property and determining that it was a corner lot, I added an extra $5,000 in market value to my existing $150,000 value. So now I determined the property to be worth $155,000. The bank was asking $95,000. I offered $85,000. The bank came back with a $93,000 counter-offer; I offered $91,000, and the bank accepted it. The real estate broker faxed me the contract with the usual bank addendum that removed all possible conventional contingencies of a normal standard contract. I had to accept the property in as-is condition, but I still obtained title insurance, so the bank had to provide me with good title (which the title company starts working on the moment we have a fully-binding contract with a projected future closing date). The bank did give me a five-day inspection period (don't expect much latitude from banks!). I used those five days to confirm my initial estimates of $11,500 (my contractor actually came back with a $9,000 estimate, but I always like to keep a bit extra for incidentals). I submitted a $1,000 deposit with my fully-executed contract to the real estate broker. It took the bank approximately four days to sign the contract (pretty common and not unusual when dealing with banks). Now I was officially under contract.

I went to work securing financing through my established cadre of hard money lenders. The real estate courses that I took had emphasized the phrase "Appraising Is an Art, not a Science." Therefore, when I determine the value of a property (in this case, $155,000), I know that five appraisers will give me five different values (maybe one will appraise at $154,000 and the other will say $156,000, and so forth).

The same holds true when a lender has to evaluate his possible loan and how much he will eventually lend. In this particular deal, I wanted to borrow 70% of the market value, or $108,500. The lender felt the property was worth only $145,000, and he wanted to lend me a maximum of $101,500. Instead of using the property equity to my advantage, this would expose me out-of-pocket, and I did not want that. You must fight for everything, even if you have to defend (in a nice way) your initial assessment of the market value. I came up with the $155,000 value because I found closed sales in the area similar to our subject property.

I printed out the comps and faxed them to the lender to prove to him that the value was there. The lender looked at the closed sales and felt more comfortable with the $155,000 valuation. (Another example of this kind of back and forth is when a bank is working on underwriting a conventional loan, the bank sometimes asks the appraiser for additional closed sales or MLS listings, or an explanation to support the value.) This is important and a good example of combining your investor hat, appraisal hat, and mortgage broker hat.

So now I had my financing in place. A week before the scheduled closing, I took a call from my title company about a few code violations. The grass was too high, and the building was unsecured. These issues are not uncommon with bank-owned homes since banks are not set up to manage property. The unsafe structure case had a lien that needed to be paid and was considered an open violation. The bank was willing to pay what was owed for the liens, but the bank was selling the property as-is. As the new buyer, I had to close out the violations. Liens can be paid, but violations may still exist.

The best way to take care of them is to just do the grunt work. I pulled a permit for the work and called the city to close out the violation with an inspection. Violations can remain on a property for a long time. They may become liens at any time, which may lead to fines. Ultimately, you can lose the property for demolition. So you must take these issues very seriously.

In most cases, you'll need to do whatever must be done to bring the property back to market condition. That was the case here. The bank paid all monies owed at the closing, but I still had violations to deal with. I had to pull a general repair permit for the boarded-up door and such. No permit had to be pulled for the high grass. All I had to do was clean up and cut the grass, and the inspector drove by and was satisfied.

The key to real estate investing is understanding what you are involved in. If the property has a lot of problems, such as physical problems, legal problems, title problems, and/or municipal and city issues, the key is to be able to understand, research, and map out the investment in the allowed contract timeline. Just because you find a property that makes sense for investment, and you put it under contract, it doesn't mean you're going to acquire and close this property; not because you don't have the money to close, but the property may have title issues and/or violations that you may or may not want to deal with. The seller may not disclose, or he may not even know that certain issues exist on his property. Having said that, the minor violations in this case weren't enough to warrant my walking away from this home.

Knowing the issues that I had to deal with, I decided to move forward, close this deal, and take the steps to put myself in an income position. Shortly after the closing, I started the renovation and the marketing simultaneously. As I mentioned in the past, all the resources around you comprise a support team for your sales force. For example, the mortgage broker helps sell your potential buyer and the contractor/handyman working on your property usually gets approached by potential buyers/tenants who live in the area or have relatives who do. When you develop a relationship with the handyman and contractor, it's always good to give incentives when they help you find potential tenants and buyers. They are not salespeople nor do you expect them to be, but you want to ensure that they point potential clients in your direction. Remember, most of the properties are distressed, and there is no telling how long they have been vacant. So once you purchase something and start renovating, people who live around the subject property become very curious about what your plans are, but they have no idea how to go about buying the property or renting it.

I consider contractors/handymen a very important conduit to any potential lead who comes around the property while they are working. I tell my contractors that if anyone appears who shows any kind of interest in a property to please call me right away on my cell phone so I can speak to the person at that moment. I cannot tell you how many properties I was able to move based on these referrals, and it's amazing to me how few investors don't think about networking with a contractor who will spend weeks or months on a property (you may never even spend that much time in your own investment property).

Here the lesson was well learned: One day while my contractor was working on the house, a woman stopped by after picking her two children up from a nearby school. She was interested in renting the home. I had prepared my contractor earlier for these kinds of questions, and he said, "Let me call the owner."

This lady happened to be a Section 8 tenant. (Section 8 is a government program that helps low-income renters by supplementing or even paying their rent. For landlords, there are advantages and disadvantages to you with this program. One advantage: You get paid in a much more secure fashion since the government pays you some or all of the rent directly. Disadvantages? You have to deal with initial inspections and annual inspections, and you're obligated to a one-year lease. Also, any government program takes a bit longer, but once you get through the red tape, you are fairly secure, and you increase your chances of avoiding non-paying tenants and evictions.)

I informed the woman that the property was for rent; as I discussed earlier, I try to rent the property and sell it at the same time. Often, when I rent a property before I sell it, I refocus my energy on selling the property to an investor with that tenant in place, and sometimes having Section 8 tenants in place makes the property more attractive for investors. As long as you buy the property at the right price (using my formulas), you will have options when you are ready to sell. You can rent the property and make money, you can sell it and make money, and you can sell it to another investor for a deep discount and still make money. I like to purchase real estate with these kinds of options; it really helps minimize my risks.

The lady liked the property so I asked her to give the deposit to my contractor; since I worked with this contractor on a regular basis and I trusted him, I was comfortable with him handling a deposit. This way I could lock the tenant in place ASAP before she found something else. Further, with a Section 8 tenant, there are some extra paperwork, forms, and procedures that, as a landlord, you'll need to handle. If you should decide to get into Section 8 rentals, you need to go to a local Section 8 office and research how it works (it may vary from state to state).

As I said earlier, it's always great to have a potential buyer or tenant already lined up with a deposit and a contract even before you finish the renovation. This can be done if you start your marketing right away.

The renovation took approximately three weeks to complete. My payments for the property were $900 a month, and the rent was $1,100 a month. This was great, but definitely not the reason I got into this property. I had set my goal of cashing in on the considerable equity I now had, equity that I owned because I had bought the property at a very favorable price.

I owned the property for three months with a tenant in place, covering my mortgage and making a bit of positive cash flow. I was still working hard to find an investor who wanted a rental property. The property was worth $155,000 as a single-family home consisting of three bedrooms and one bath. I marketed the property for $149,900 with a 3% seller contribution toward the closing costs. Again, my strategy is to keep turning properties over. Make a profit and move on. Much depends on the market and how long you're willing to wait until you find a buyer. (You don't have to agree with this, or do the same thing on every investment. I approach advice like supermarket shopping; you walk around supermarket aisles, take what you want, and leave on the shelf what you don't like. That's how I think you should handle advice in general.)

If you fall in love with a property and it makes sense to keep it and rent it, you might refinance the home and put a conventional mortgage on it (taking the hard money lender out of the temporary loan). My objective on this property was to turn it over quickly. I like to have an edge over my competition and try to do a little bit more than another seller is willing to do, whatever will bring me a buyer faster.

I ran an ad in the local paper: Investment property, already rented, with a Sec 8 tenant in place. Seller willing to help with closing costs.

As you know, you need to understand the mortgage business. Hopefully, by now you understand that there are many programs in which the lenders allow the seller to contribute a certain percentage of the sales price toward the buyer's closing costs (which varies from buyer to buyer and bank to bank).

I received a lot of calls from my ad. I used my consulting selling method when dealing with potential buyers. When I spoke to potential buyers (and put my salesperson hat on), I asked questions that told me who they are: Questions such as, "Are you a full-time investor? Are you doing this part-time? Have you ever bought a property before? How much money are you working with? Are you looking to live in the property?" Again, do not forget my grandmother's philosophy, that God gave you two ears and one mouth. Do you think He was trying to tell you something?

I needed to ask a lot of questions and do a lot of listening to know what kind of buyers I was dealing with, what they were looking for. You need to determine that what you have will work for them.

Then you need to wait to see who takes action.

Let me explain. You need to work with people who are willing to follow your lead and heed your advice. For example, if you tell them to get pre-qualified with a mortgage broker and they do it, that's a good indication that they're serious. If you get an address and tell them to drive by and they do it, that's another good indication that they're serious. These are the kind of buyers that you want to work with so you don't waste your TIME.

Keep in mind that you don't want to disturb the tenants every time you have a potential buyer. Tenants may get nervous when they see you marketing the property, and they fear they will have to move. This fear sometimes triggers a move even though they don't really have to. You may lose a tenant, so unless you have a serious buyer who is willing to keep the tenants for the duration of the lease, don't start sending people in and disturbing the tenants until you've solidly qualified each buyer.

I soon had found a buyer who followed the steps I had asked him to take and showed a genuine desire to make the purchase. I was asking $149,900, he offered me $140,000, and we eventually settled on a price of $145,000. I wrote a contract with a 45-day closing. The buyer had his own mortgage broker he was working with. I always like to speak to the mortgage broker just to make sure he is qualified to do the loan (not all mortgage brokers are created equal!). I was not favorably impressed with this mortgage broker, but the broker was the buyer's cousin, and it was tough for me to push him out of the equation; it was something I could live with if the broker didn't push the closing period out past the agreed-upon 45 days. Hoping for the best, I put the property under contract and took it off the market. I had now owned the property for four months. I wasn't prepared for what happened next.

I received a letter from the city. It was a warning about a code violation for a property with uncut grass and in general disrepair. Of course, this was quite a surprise as I thought I had brought all violations up to code months before. I assumed it was a simple clerical error. I called the city inspector to clear this up, but the property he described was substantially different from the one I owned.

I drove to the property and found myself quite shocked. When I had first looked at this property, I saw a single-family home on the corner, completely fenced. The property description indicated that this lot was zoned duplex, but the zoning only indicated what could be built on this lot, not necessarily what had been built. In other words, an owner could have built a duplex but did not have to; he or she might have chosen to build a single-family home, regardless of the zoning. With the mix of single-family and multi-family homes in the neighborhood, anything could have happened.

But now, when I looked to the right of my home I spotted another single-family home just north of my subject property. I had not paid attention to this building during my first inspection because both homes were separately fenced. I had no indication that this second home was part of my property. But the city called and demanded that I clean up my lot and mow the grass. Hadn't I done that? Yes, or so I thought. Now, looking over what I had thought to be an adjacent property, I saw tall grass and a rough lot. Could that be part of my property? After all, the county, when they saw a code violation, had pulled my name as the owner.

I pulled the tax record out of my briefcase: zoned duplex, which meant there could be two homes on one lot, and then lot size; the given size in the tax roll seemed much bigger than the lot my "one" home occupied.

I grabbed my cell phone and called the city building inspector in charge.

"I received a letter about a lawn violation on one of my properties. Could you please describe the building on the lot you saw? Do you remember the color?"

"How can I forget?" the building inspector said. "It was a gruesome green color."

Now I began to realize that the second home was almost certainly on my lot! I thanked the inspector and hung up my cell phone. Then I stared across at the gruesome green home that I now realized was a second home on my lot—one I didn't even know I had.

Now, you might ask: Didn't the seller describe the property to you? Understand, when you're buying a property from a bank the officer in charge of signing the contract from the bank has probably never even seen the property. Remember, you are dealing with unconventional real estate; therefore, you have unconventional circumstances, some favorable to you and some unfavorable.

In this case, my investment changed completely, in many ways for the better. I ended up with another property that needed some renovation; nothing crazy, probably $4,000 in repairs. Even better, I controlled a duplex worth not the $155,000 I calculated earlier, but $190,000. This sounds crazy, I know, but this is what happened!

So where was I now? I not only had two single-family homes rather than one, but they stood on a lot that constituted a legal "duplex" and could not be subdivided for separate sale. Further, I had a buyer lined up to purchase a property at below market value—now considerably below market value, considering that I now had two homes on the lot! The buyer, at any rate, was using bank financing, which meant the other home would have to be renovated and brought up to code. This all would take time.

I gave the buyer a choice of paying more for the property or walking away with a refund of his deposit in hand. The buyer preferred to purchase a property that would close sooner than I now could, so he chose to bow out. Most important, the startling new developments caused a change in my strategy. The property, and the increased rent that it would bring, now looked like an excellent long-term hold-and-rent investment. I found myself even more excited about the investment since I learned the big news that I owned two investment properties in one (and for the price of one). I wanted to keep the property because of the significant cash flow it would return.

The second home was about half the size of the first home on the lot. I painted inside and out, repaired a few windows, put in a new kitchen and vanity, and carpeted throughout. The whole project cost $3,500 in additional work.

Remember, I've told you to network with everyone in the area about any property you want to sell or rent. Again, my rule paid off. I rented the second home to a friend of my first renter. The second home rented for $600, which put me in an excellent cash flow position. Then I refinanced the property with a conventional 20-year loan of

$120,000. To this day, the property is rented, and I'm enjoying a positive cash flow.

Here are some lessons from this transaction:

When you meet possible contacts for your business

Learn to distinguish which ones are worth following up with on regular basis.

When you get a lead, time is of the essence

So make sure you get back to people fast. It's a great way to overcome the competition.

Learn the tax record system

It is very important to be able to make the right decisions day in and day out.

Be involved in every aspect of your transaction

The buy, the sale, the renovation, the mortgage process—during your sale.

Learn to adapt different property management strategies

Depending on the type of property and neighborhood you are investing in.

Learn to utilize your immediate sphere of influence

Case Study Seven

The Bermuda Triangle of Contractors

As I went through my usual contacts one morning, I phoned one of my investors, who told me she had recently purchased a property and was looking to wholesale it. She was asking $125,000. She told me the property was a duplex, but the previous owners had manipulated the floor plan and turned it into four rentable units. I took down the address and basic information and started working on my research.

The tax record showed that this property was zoned as a duplex, which meant it was not in compliance as a four-plex. There were sales in the area for $300,000 and up. This was definitely something of interest and was worth looking at physically.

I had a decent relationship with the seller, so told her I needed 24 hours, and asked her not to do anything until she heard from me. I always try to protect my time as best I can, and I hate learning that property is no longer available after I have put time into researching it. I've seen so many new investors putting days or even weeks of effort into a possible deal, only to find out it's no longer available by the time they are ready to make an offer. If you come across a promising deal, chances are there is a limit on how long it will stay on the market. Always remember that.

As I drove to the property, I noted that the area was a mixed-use location, with business and residential properties near a major street, all in all, a good location. However, one thing did worry me. I noticed that the original floor plan had been altered. When you buy a property, you are inheriting every quirky renovation that has been completed before you arrived. The seller did not put work into the house and wasn't planning on it. His intention was to sell it for a discount in an "as-is" condition to another investor. I had no way to learn the history of this property and why it had been changed to the four-plex floor plan it now had.

When I encounter a structure that has been redesigned, I do all I can to discover the original floor plan. Then I determine what changes have been made. Here, the original structures consisted of one detached home in front and another in rear. The front structure was fairly large, approximately 1,800 sq. ft., and the back structure was much smaller, closer to 600 sq. ft. The previous owner had broken the front building up into three separate units while keeping the back structure as one unit. This allowed him two additional income opportunities (rental units). I could understand why somebody would want to get the most out of his space.

The current owner had purchased this property from a bank. This told me that this property was originally in foreclosure, went back to the bank as a result, and was sold through a Realtor/agent to the current owner. The property needed quite a bit of work but nothing unusual, so this did not worry me. I was more concerned about what to do with the modified floor plan.

So during my first visit to the property, I had to be able to decide what work I would have to do to the property and how I was going to handle the breakup of the rental opportunities. I also had to decide how much money this would cost me since I was still in the process of determining if this investment was good for me.

I felt the best tack was to make the front structure into two large units rather than three units. I decided to leave the back as one unit.

The result was a lot of work to be done. All the units needed new kitchens and new bathrooms, some walls needed to be removed, we had to update the electrical components, we had to paint the units inside and out, and it needed basic flooring. I estimated the renovation to be $25,000.

My choice of floor plans meant the property would constitute a three-unit rental rather than four. Even though this property was legally a duplex, it was still in a multi-family area. I was allowed to have up to four units as long as they were up to code and done correctly to the city's specifications.

I now had to peg the actual market value. This was an investment area—a neighborhood with many closed sales and listed properties and new construction. (When you're looking at analyzing market values, make sure your appraiser hat is on.) Keep in mind with investment areas that people will be buying low and selling high. You should consider the actual retail cost of a house, not wholesale. There will be other investors just like you buying under market value. So you need to be able to distinguish between the investor sales and actual retail sales. To accomplish this, I look for at least six sales that are comparable to my property. I always use the six highest comparables in any given neighborhood. The lower sales in an investor neighborhood are probably just that—investment properties. There will be a lot of low sales in an active investment area; don't let these low-end sales discourage you, because they might represent a number of extreme examples of distressed properties. Focus your findings from the tax record on the higher-end sales rather than pulling your averages down with some of these oddball investor sales. Many new investors have a tendency to look at one extreme or the other, which may discourage them from pursuing what could be a great opportunity.

But again, appraising is an art, not a science. So when you do an appraisal, you need to consider the condition of the lower-priced properties. More often than not, those properties are not in market condition, and making sure "comps" are as similar as possible is vital. If you have a lot of sales at the $300,000+ level, there is no need to search for other sales. Take the highest value in the subdivision, rather than using the lowball sales, which will drive down your average. In this instance, even though I found a lot of low sales, I also saw many high sales. I took the time to drive to six different houses that I had used in my comparisons to look at the condition, neighborhood, and the type of property. These aspects are very important to examine, because they help determine the true market value and are vital to your final purchase decision.

To determine the market value when you are analyzing

a property that has all types of values, you need to research by comparables, not necessarily by the cash flow method. For example, if you are analyzing an apartment building, you will typically examine cash flow. But when you analyze mixed use (single family, multi-family, business) in an active investor area, you will check the comparables. (From time to time, I get calls from appraisers doing this same kind of work, wanting to know the condition of the property I sold and what kind of work was put into the property before sale.) Remember, if you are not comfortable with assessing a value, just call an appraiser and get his opinion.

So after doing my research on the true market value, I determined the property to be worth $325,000. Going back to my formula, I multiplied $325,000 by 70%, which is $227,500. I subtracted the $25,000 for renovation, which is $202,500. I also took an additional $20,000 off for closing costs and holding time, which is $182,500. That would be the most I could pay for the property. Since the asking price was $125,000, I was in very good shape.

I called the investors for the property and told them I was interested and would be sending an offer shortly. I offered the full asking price; the numbers were right, and I did not want to chance losing this property. I did not want to make a lower offer and waste time negotiating only to have somebody else drive up the price. I have lost great deals in the past, when, wasting time trying to get a better price during my negotiating process with the seller, another buyer came and either out-bid me or drove up the price. So here I offered the full asking price and put the property under contract.

Since this was a big renovation, I wanted the right person for the repair work. I had three contractors in my Rolodex I liked to work with on a regular basis and another with whom I had not previously worked. I like to simultaneously work on my financing and renovation estimates the moment I put the property under contract. Time is of the essence so I have to have things lined up. As I am working on getting bids for renovation, I also ask a few lenders to give me estimates on a loan amount. I was asking for a $165,000 loan, and since the property was worth $300,000, I felt pretty comfortable with my request. Since my original estimate for renovation was $25,000, I was trying to get close or even less than this in case of a rainy day.

When it came to the renovation part of this deal, I learned what the school of hard knocks means. I learned that you get what you pay for. I always say that only rich people can afford to do things cheaply because they can afford to do it over again. I had two estimates for the remodel. One was for $21,000, and the other one was for $23,000. But the new contractor I had not yet used gave me an estimate for $16,000. The temptation of spending $7,000 less on the renovation was too much. I decided to use the new handyman for this particular project.

Since I was purchasing the property at such a great deal, getting a loan was not challenging for this particular situation. I quickly had the loan lined up for $165,000 as well as a handyman to do the work. All I waited for was the title to be ready so I could coordinate the closing. Soon we had a title and a closing, and I was ready to begin.

Shortly after the closing, the renovation was underway. I gave the handyman a $5,000 retainer to start the job. Three weeks after the work began, he approached me and informed me that he had underbid the project and would not be able to do it for $16,000. This is not the situation I wanted to be in, so I asked how much more money he needed to finalize the project. He told me he needed $2,000 more. Since $18,000 was still below budget, I agreed to the increase but decided to keep a sharp eye on him to make sure he was done on time. I also gave him an additional $5,000 toward the renovation, totaling a retainer of $10,000. I started going to the property on a regular basis to check on his progress, but I soon noticed the rehab was not moving forward at the pace I expected. I felt this handyman could not get the job done in time, and I also anticipated he would be hitting me up for more money again. So I decided before things got out of hand to end my relationship with him and let somebody else more reliable finish the job. The quote from my new contractor to finish the job was $12,000. Since I had already spent $10,000, I was still below budget; now I had a little bit more peace of mind that this job would be completed on time. Anybody who's ever been involved in renovation work knows that you will encounter delays. As an investor, your salesman hat doesn't come off when you're dealing with contractors. I wanted to make the transition from one contractor to the next as easy as possible. I didn't want to upset my current contractor.

I also did not want to burn any bridges with him and risk him filing complaints against my property. To salvage our relationship and protect my property, I resorted to a bit of a white lie: I informed him that another handyman was going to purchase the property (he was not), and one of the buyer's requests was that he finish the work himself. This allowed me to save face with the initial contractor and have no hard feelings. To just fire him was not a chance I wanted to take.

This approach allowed me to maintain a smooth transition with no hard feelings. My new contractor finished the job within the next three weeks.

Here is an overview of how this property looked the first time I viewed it, and then how it appeared when completely renovated.

Of course, the front property was originally very rough. The previous owner, it seemed to me, was trying to maximize income with no regard for the esthetics of the property. The living space had been divided up into many small rooms. The exteriors were very dilapidated. A back room that was now being used as a bedroom had originally been used a laundry room (I spotted dryer hookups!). The back building was a very small detached home; although the flooring wasn't bad, the kitchen, bathroom, and roof needed replacing. Further, a wood shed had been put up between the two buildings.

When renovations were completed, I had opened up the floor plan on the front structure by reducing the three units to two units. I was able to increase the size of each unit. Each unit now had a brand-new kitchen. A drop ceiling, the type often seen in office buildings to cover the mechanicals, had been torn out, which opened up the room and provided more light and space. I converted the tiny back "bedroom" into a laundry room—its originally intended use. The rental units now had their own private Laundromat.

The old shed between the buildings had been demolished. In the back building, the roof was now new and leak-free; the new kitchen was L-shaped, with white cabinets at floor and ceiling. The lawn area featured fresh sod with red mulch at the edges. A new walkway made from red paver bricks led to the front door of the front building and then around the front building to the door of the rear building.

Both buildings wore a fresh coat of peach-colored paint,

all trimmed white around windows and doors. The cyclone fence surrounding the property had been replaced with a wooden fence to help improve the look of the area.

I started my marketing right away. Now, in this particular case the buyer might live in one of the units and rent out the others. When you're selling a property, you want to describe how a prospect might buy the property and how he or she will use it to their advantage. I ran an ad in the paper that said this triplex would be great for someone to live in. I also added that the seller would help with closing costs. If you were a buyer, would this interest you? Few real estate ads read like this. When the ad ran, I received a very large response. But never forget: You can get a lot of calls and a lot of interest, but the percentage to actually come through is very small. Real estate is definitely a numbers game, and you need to know how to handle calls as they come in. Try to explain and communicate as best you can with the potential buyer. Make it as easy and as accessible as possible to purchase your property. Then you can work with those who do what you ask. If you ask a lead to go look at the property and give you feedback and he or she does as you say, this is a good indication that he or she is serious. If you ask someone to call you back or call the mortgage broker and get prequalified and he or she does it without hesitation, that's another indication that he or she is serious.

I ran the ad for three weeks. I must've gotten more than a hundred phone calls. Of the hundred calls, only 10 people seemed truly interested. Of those 10, only five people got prequalified. And out of those five, only two were actually preapproved. Finally, only one gave me a deposit.

Using one of my favorite selling techniques, I offered a contribution toward the buyer's closing costs (subject to lender approval). The sale price was $325,000, and I would contribute 6% toward closing. This left me with a net before my closing costs of $305,500. I signed a contract and started moving toward closing. It had been four months from the moment I purchased the property to the moment the selling contract was signed. The buyer was qualified for 90% of the purchase price. He had to put the other 10% down, which in this case was about $30,000.

Unfortunately, a few days before the scheduled closing, the buyer informed me that he had fallen into some hardship and had only $15,000, not the $30,000 needed to purchase the property. I had been working on this closing hard and looking forward to a very nice potential profit. I was into the property for about $175,000 and was anticipating a $125,000 gain. So after speaking to the bank and the mortgage broker, I had to make an adjustment and hold a second mortgage, with the bank's approval, for the $15,000 that the buyer did not have.

Once you have a closing on the table and there is money to be made, you want to do whatever it takes to close. Instead of making $125,000, I ended up making $110,000, definitely still a good scenario. A lot of investors would get greedy and decide they want to go for the $125,000 profit. I can't count how many times in either buying or selling I had to control my greed and put it on the back burner and focus on the business aspect of the deal, not the emotional part of it. Every day that went by, I was racking up mortgage expenses, plus taxes and insurance, so not closing on the deal meant slowly losing money every day. So the right play was to close and move on. Even if the buyer defaulted on the second mortgage, I was still okay with it, because the upfront money that I made was sufficient enough for me. I guess you can call me a "cup is half–full" kind of guy when it comes to business.

Here are some lessons from this transaction:

Not wasting time is key

When a potential seller calls you about a possible investment, you want to make sure that you move swiftly.

Remember, when you buy a property you are inheriting everything about that property

Good or bad. Do your homework and stay out of trouble.

Try to work with competent contractors.

The people skills that you acquire will always serve you in business and in life

As a business owner, you need to learn to manage people and learn to make good transition.

Don't be greedy; use the velocity of money to keep turning over deals

Case Study Eight

Converting a Tenant to a Buyer

Earlier, we discussed different "wells" that you can go to purchase real estate. These are different sources of acquisitions. HUD is a vast well that you can turn to in your search for solid real estate investments.

HUD offers one- to four-unit residential properties acquired as a result of a foreclosure action on an FHA-insured mortgage (more on FHA in a moment). HUD becomes the property owner and offers the property for sale to recover the loss on the foreclosure claim. There are a lot of different programs out there for mortgages. The government plays a major role in some of these sponsorships of loans.

What about the FHA? FHA stands for the Federal Housing Administration, which is a program that helps first-time homebuyers purchase homes with little money down. There is a maximum loan amount for this program, as well as guidelines that must be adhered to. The most important aspect of these loans is that the federal government insures the loans that banks make. This simply means that the government will guarantee any loan by a member bank that suffers a default. So if a member bank lends, say, $150,000 for an FHA mortgage and the borrower defaults, the government will buy that loan from the bank and take possession of the subject property. The idea is that the bank assumes very little risk for approving this type of government-guaranteed loan.

Once HUD seizes a property, HUD sells it through closed-auction bidding, wherein all properties available for purchase by the public are offered for sale at Internet listing sites maintained by management companies under contract to HUD. Any real estate broker registered with HUD may submit an offer and contract to purchase on your behalf. HUD pays the real estate broker's commission, if included in the contract. An interested bidder must make an offer within a specific deadline, no one knows what anybody else bids, and after the deadline, the highest bidder gets the property. This is similar to a traditional auction, but with no auctioneer talking at 100 mph or a crowd making verbal offers aloud. Everybody makes his or her highest and best offer "blind" with just one shot at it.

HUD homes sell throughout the country, so ask your local Realtor or research the Internet to find out about what is available and how to bid on HUD homes.

Properties listed with HUD change on a regular basis, so it is a very good source of inventory. But the same investor rules apply: stay consistent and follow up. This is a very important aspect to being successful in this environment. Throughout my investing career, I have purchased many properties through HUD and VA (through the Veterans Authority, which works the same way as HUD; it's a program dedicated specifically for retired veterans' loans that go bad). As long as you do your homework and you stay consistent and constantly make offers, you will find success.

One afternoon, I was following my prescribed property search routine and reading through the HUD listings. This particular week, there were five properties for sale. When it comes to HUD offerings, I try to make an offer on every single acceptable property, regardless of what they are asking. Don't forget, this is a numbers game, and you need to throw as much mud at the wall as you possibly can to see what sticks. The list came out on a Monday with the bidding deadline set for midnight of the following Sunday. In these auctions, the asking price is on the list, which is a very helpful starting point. HUD displays a picture of the property and puts the inspection report on the Web site, along with some other basic property information.

I printed out the available properties: four single-family homes and one duplex. I looked up the market value on all five, looked at the basic remarks on the renovation costs, and looked at their asking prices.

Based on that information, I tried to narrow down which properties I could be in contention with and which ones I could aggressively go after when I make my offer. Since this is a highest-and- best-offer bidding situation, you want to make the most of it and offer the top amount you are willing to pay for each property (remember you are not negotiating with a seller in this case). In this example, I was not dealing with an agent or another investor, so the professional relationships and personal connections that I had cultivated were not going to give me any advantages. There were no favorites here; it was strictly numbers.

I compared their asking prices to the market values. I wanted to give myself the best chances for winning the properties by bidding very close to their asking price or even higher. So after looking at all five properties, I found two properties that were priced right and one that I felt would give me a good chance to make a strong run at it. I still made low-ball offers on the other three but with little expectation that I would win. But you never know, and as long as these were conservative offers, I had little to lose. After being in this business for a while, you start to have a gut feel for what you think would be a good buy. That feeling comes with experience, educating yourself, and the desire to constantly learn.

Let's talk about the two deals I looked at. The first was a three-bedroom, two-bath single-family home. My research indicated that the market value was $140,000. They were asking $80,000. The other property was a two-bedroom, two-bath single-family home with a market value of $150,000 for which they were asking $75,000. I got in my car and drove to the properties.

The first, the three-bedroom, two-bath home for $80,000, was on a nice street. The home had been built in the 1960s, and all the homes around the subject property were built during the same period. I walked around the property and looked inside. The property had basic cosmetic needs, such as some window work, paint inside and out, and flooring. I estimated the home needed $12,000 in renovation. Then I drove to the second property, a two-bedroom, two-bath single-family home priced at $75,000. This was a nice single-family home! It was not a big house, but it had a solid appeal and a lovely lot that was fenced all around. One thing that I noticed was that some of the empty lots on the street had been purchased by other investors and new construction homes were being built all around the subject property. This was a very positive factor because it told me that the neighborhood was up-and-coming and people here were investing in the future. Unlike the first home, the two-bedroom, two-bath home was not in heavy disrepair and needed only $6,000 in renovation. The kitchen was good, the bathrooms were sound; it basically needed paint inside and out, some tile and carpeting, and cleanup. I now was ready to get back to my office and get to work.

One good thing about bidding through HUD is that nobody could buy out from underneath me; in other words, everybody had to wait until midnight on Sunday (or whichever dateline HUD dictates). I could take my time and make sure I completed all my due diligence and made the safest decision possible. Unlike when buying it from an investor or a Realtor, I didn't have to exercise some of the urgency that I'd had to in the past. As I pulled up the list on Monday, I had six days to do my research and make my offer.

So let's look at deal number one: the $80,000, three-bedroom, two-bath home that I felt was worth $140,000 and needed $12,000 in work. Going back to my trusty formula, 70% of $140,000 is $98,000. I subtract $12,000 in renovation, less another $12,000 in holding time and closing costs, which meant I should try to purchase this property for $74,000. HUD was asking $80,000 so I decided to make an offer for $75,000, or $5,000 less than what they were asking.

The remaining property was the two-bedroom, two-bath single-family home. HUD was asking $75,000, and I thought the property was worth $150,000, less my renovation costs of $6,000. So 70% of $150,000 is $105,000, subtract $6,000 in renovation and an additional $12,000 for closing costs and holding time, and my purchase price should be no more than $87,000. They were asking $75,000 so I had plenty of room to be a bit more aggressive. I decided to offer $80,000, $5,000 more than the asking price. I made the offers on a Friday and noted on my calendar to look for the results on the Monday to follow.

When the time came, I did not win either home! So why am I mentioning this case? Because the deal is never done until there is an actual closing. Here is a very important lesson: Just because somebody else offered more than you or beat you to a deal, it doesn't mean that person is actually going to close. You should only worry about what you can control, not those issues over which you have no control. This is a very important lesson to understand in business and in life. I have researched many, many deals that I could not buy in the end. But a percentage of those deals ended up coming back because the person who originally won the bid could not close for one reason or another.

Having said that, when you win a bid in this particular example (HUD), you need to submit paperwork, a deposit, and actually purchase the property within the allocated time (which is usually 45 days). If you don't, you lose your deposit, and HUD goes to the next bidder and offers him or her the opportunity to purchase the property.

Still, I was disappointed. It would have been easy for me to allow crazy thoughts to go through my head: "I should have bid more, I should have, could have—" It's far better, though, not to worry about things that you cannot control, and you certainly can't change the past! You can't change something that happened five seconds ago, or five years ago, so a minimum amount of energy should be dedicated to damage assessment. Analyze the past only as a way to improve your future results; don't let it sap your energy and positive attitude.

I didn't drive myself nuts with second-guessing, but stuck to my carefully plotted-out bid numbers. I had decided how much I should pay and there was no reason for me to deviate from those carefully considered numbers. In business, any unnecessary emotional involvement will just compromise your ability to make sound decisions.

You've probably guessed what happened next. Three weeks later, I got a call from HUD offering me the property at my original $80,000 bid! I was excited. This was very motivating, and it reinforced that I should never give up or allow my morale to sink. These things happen every day in this business. I submitted all the necessary paperwork, and within a couple of days, I received confirmation that I was officially under contract to purchase the property.

Let's revisit my original assessment of the property. I always put my salesman hat on and try to picture who would be the perfect client for this home. I felt certain this particular house (the two-bedroom, two-bath) would be a great home for a first-time homebuyer. It had great curb appeal and a very nice yard. And the many new homes being built around the neighborhood really helped spruce up the look of the area. So I felt strongly about finding a buyer who would want to live in this property rather than selling it to an investor for a wholesale price.

Because this house was not in terrible shape, I could apply for conventional bank financing rather than going through my private lenders. However, I still chose to use the private lenders. Conventional lenders take up to 45 days. I did not want to lose this deal. I preferred not to cut it so close. When it's time to purchase a property, you want to put yourself in position to close. You work so hard to find the right deal that you don't want to get caught up with red tape and lose the property and your deposit because a bank is taking its good old time to underwrite your loan.

Further, with conventional financing I would be required to use my own money for a down payment and for closing costs. Even though I could get a better interest rate with conventional financing (the private lenders were charging double-digit interest rates), the fact that I would not have to put up as much of my own money to get a private loan superseded the negative of the double-digit interest rate.

So I went to my hard money lender contacts requesting a loan amount of $105,000 for a property that is worth $150,000. After a few of them got back to me, the best I could borrow was $101,000. I accepted it, and we went to closing.

Since this was a very light renovation, I started thinking about strategy and planning how I was going to market the property. I decided that the best way to market this property would be to promote it as a rental with an option to buy. Sometimes, if you strictly promote a property as "for sale," the sticker price may intimidate buyers. Most people, especially first-time homebuyers, don't understand real estate. Many buyers can actually qualify for a home, but just don't know it. So, I actually promoted this house as a rental even though I had no intention of renting this property long-term. How does this work? I was asking $1,200 a month for rent. And the fact of the matter is, that would also be the mortgage amount. So anybody calling to rent the property could in reality afford the monthly mortgage. I could help with closing costs and give him or her an option to buy within months. I might also apply a portion of the rent toward the down payment, so it's almost a no-brainer and just a matter of finding the right buyer to understand it and qualify.

Think about it: You are a tenant looking to rent a property for $1,200 a month, and your first, last, and security totals $3,600 (this being your move-in cost for renting), and I am willing to apply a half of each month's rent for a specific amount of time toward your purchase price. So when it's time to purchase the property you have few little out-of-pocket expenses, and you own the home you already live in. At the same time, you needn't worry about moving again, and can take advantage of being a homeowner, enjoying all the tax advantages that homeowners have. It almost sounds too good to be true, but it's that simple. Looking at it from my point of view (the owner), I set aside some of the monies that I received to go toward closing costs and down payment, and I make a sale. Sometimes pitching this is smoother and easier to digest than a straight sale. I've sold many homes through this strategy, so I decided to market the property to a tenant. Once people contacted me, I would explain to them the wonderful option that they now had. Most people get very excited when you tell them that they can now buy a home with the same amount of money that they pour into a mere rental. Doing all this changes little, except that the seller is willing to be flexible and give the renter an opportunity to be homeowner.

I have always viewed real estate selling as solving a problem and offering a solution, rather than hard-core selling. After talking to dozens of potential tenants/buyers, I found a couple who were excited about what I had to say. When I talk to potential buyers, my number one objective is to establish that they love the house and want to live here. When you are dealing with a potential homeowner/retail buyer, it is great that the numbers are attractive, but they *need to like the home*. Of course, the price has to be right. So, as a salesperson you must find somebody who will fall in love with the home. Once you do, the potential buyer/tenant will be motivated and willing to do whatever it takes to purchase the house.

Since I was running an ad to find potential tenants/buyers, and since they were calling me directly, they were probably not working with a mortgage broker. This gave me the opportunity to not only rent my property but also to find a buyer who would use my mortgage broker to do the deal. That was a lot of pluses. After a couple of weeks of taking dozens of calls, I found a husband and a wife who had one daughter. The wife was an administrative assistant for a car dealership, and the husband worked for a construction company. In them, I had found two hard-working adults who could afford the monthly payment but did not make enough money to save the down payment and closing costs that it usually took to purchase a home. They found themselves constantly moving because renting on an annual basis gave them a bit of uncertainty each year. (Another thing to keep in mind: Not only do you need to find tenants who are willing and have the desire to be homeowners, but they also need to be able to qualify for the home, as you'll soon see.)

After a few conversations and a couple of visits to the property, they were ready to make the move and rent with the option to buy my property. This part is very important: I needed to be able to qualify them before they moved into the property. I certainly don't want to move them into the property, find out they can't qualify, and then have to move them out. My mortgage broker contacted them so he could start qualifying them for future acquisition. Unfortunately, their credit wasn't strong enough to purchase.

Let me give you a quick synopsis of what it takes to purchase a home, as this is very important. To purchase a home, you need three things: credit, income, and cash. They had the income, and they had the cash (the first, last, and security). Plus, I was going to rent to them and apply a portion of their rent toward the purchase. But their credit, due to some prior derogatory, was too low to qualify for a loan.

Here I learned anew: Don't stop there. I had found good people ready to go, but they fell just short with their credit. So I asked them if they had family members or friends whom they trusted who might be willing to help. Co-signers are used all the time in homes, cars, credit cards, and anything credit-related. When I got my first credit card, my mother co-signed with me (since I was young and had no credit history). That gave me an opportunity to get my foot in the door and start building my own credit. When you are trying to sell to someone, you are educating and selling him or her at the same time. This was a perfect example of the art of educating and selling at the same time. They had an aunt living in another state who was willing to help. We got in touch with the aunt, pre-qualified her, and she co-signed with the couple and helped them purchase the home.

I had to rent to them for eight months to put away enough toward the loan down payment. So even though I rented to them for $1,200 a month, I kept $600 and applied the other $600 toward their purchase. My payments were $900 a month, and I was pocketing only $600. So I was out-of-pocket $300 month or $2,400 until closing. But I did pick up $3,600 when they moved in, which means I still made $1,200 during those eight months. When it was time for the closing, I sold the property for $150,000 less $5,000 in closing costs. So I took in $145,000, minus my payoff and my expenses of $102,000, netting a profit of $43,000. Not bad! This is what I call a "soft approach" to selling and my "tenant conversion to buyer" approach. It's very effective, and it helps you and your buyer. There is no better way to make a profit than when you are helping someone at the same time.

Here are some lessons from this transaction:

No deals are off the market until they close

Use the rent-to-own strategy to find your buyer

Solving somebody's problem is a great way to sell—it's a win-win scenario

When selling to a retail buyer, first you must establish that he or she likes the home before you do *anything*; don't waste time focusing on the numbers until the person wants to be in the property.

Case Study Nine

How I Went to a New Town and Purchased a Property in Three Hours

Using the knowledge acquired in real estate is key, and you may learn to apply it in any market. As I mentioned earlier, the most effective way to be successful is to network. As you become successful, people gravitate to you. Understanding the business you're in and how to successfully create business marriages will grow your business.

As I established myself in South Florida and settled into the market, I started looking elsewhere to invest. In order to move into another market, you need to have the right people in place. As you are reading this book, realize what it takes to be successful in this business. Think of the time, effort, knowledge, and money it takes to put it all together. I can't be in two places at once, so I decided to start looking for key individuals I could start working with to expand my marketplace. It's not easy to find a person whom you can trust, have a good chemistry with, and feel that he or she fits the character and personality that it takes to be successful in this business.

When you are focused on a specific task in your life, you tend to talk about it a lot to your family and friends. This is especially true in real estate, which is exciting, lucrative, and fascinating to most people. Almost everybody wants to be part of it, especially if one demonstrates success.

I started looking around for people to involve in my business to allow me to leverage my time. I first looked at my sphere of influence. Those were my friends, family members, and people I had done business with. I had a very close friend who was living in the Northeast section of the United States and teaching at our old high school. Of course, we talked on a regular basis on a social level. But as I became successful, others couldn't help notice the lifestyle change that I was experiencing. So, one evening in a passing conversation I mentioned that I was looking for someone to help me expand to a new market. Even though he loved teaching, he was also motivated and interested in growing and diversifying and doing something bigger. He decided to move on and get out of teaching and into the real estate business under my wing.

We are all forced to make decisions every day, and it is not always clear which is the right one. When my friend chose to move, he informed his colleagues at the school, who were nothing but supportive. You see, my friend had only been teaching for a short time, while many of his colleagues had been teaching for 15 years or more. Every single teacher with years of experience reinforced to him that he was making the right decision. Even if you don't understand what you're about to get into, people with seniority and more life experience can help you make the right call. So he packed his stuff and moved. I entered a new marketplace. This brings me to the next deal. I will show you how I flew to the new market for 24 hours, and we found a deal and put it under contract—all during my one day trip.

Once you understand how to analyze deals, you start to recognize good opportunities from bad ones no matter where you are. I got into town at about 10 a.m., and we started working immediately. I was still in the teaching mode, but at the same time looking for opportunities in the new marketplace. We sat down and started to go over the checklist and started looking at all the ways that there is to buy. I put my investor hat on and started researching leads to analyze. I took the time to fly into the new market, and I wanted to take full advantage of my time and hopefully, in the process, find a good buy and plant a seed that would hopefully pay off down the road. We started looking in a multi-listing service. I started to eyeball some available properties for sale. I searched a specific area, which I identified as our potential farm area and looked at what was available for sale.

When I'm searching an MLS, I like to look at a few key things.

First, I like to look at the remarks and how the seller is describing his or her property. For example, if the property description states that the property is in "move-in condition, bring your toothbrush," that is not a good indication for an investor. Why do I say this? Because the majority of the time, heavily discounted properties will require some level of renovation. "Bring a toothbrush" means everything is probably up to date, modern, and ready to go. (More on this in "A Quick Lesson" at the end of this chapter.)

So as I was searching the MLS, I saw one property that popped out. They were asking only $30,000. To me, that seemed interesting right off the bat. So I started researching the property and looking at the tax roll. This was a small single-family home with a decent-sized lot, and there were plenty of sales in the area between $80,000 and $85,000. This property, on the surface and on paper, looked interesting so we decided to get in the car and check out the property as soon as possible.

But before I even got into my car, I sent over a letter of intent offering $27,000, even though I hadn't seen the property. Sound risky? Not at all. I made the offer with a three-day inspection. If the seller accepted my offer, I would still have an out. I wouldn't lose any deposit money. The purpose of doing this was to hold the property so I wouldn't waste any time if someone else made an offer. And since this property was priced right already I was afraid to lose the property to competition, so I needed to get a jump on any potential competitors. Aggressiveness and a sense of urgency were key here. If something is truly a good deal, chances are it will not last long. So you must move with a sense of urgency. I wanted the ball in my court, so the decision would be mine and not dictated by mere chance.

So we faxed over the offer and then drove to the property. As we approached the property, we could tell it was definitely in disrepair and in need of work. The first thing I did was walk around the property and the outside perimeter. I was putting on my salesperson hat already. I was trying to imagine what kind of buyer I would have.

The positive part of this house was that it was cheap and the payments to the future homeowner would be affordable. To me, that single point would make this a good turnover-type property, because most people would be able to afford it with a selling price in the $85,000 range. Their payments would be under $1,000 a month, which would be the same as renting, or less. So using my used car sales method, I would be trying to sell a payment, rather than a sales price. I entered the property and noticed it needed paint inside and out, new carpeting throughout the home, new kitchen, and a new bathroom. The roof was in good shape, and the house had decent curb appeal. My objective here was to be able to rapidly determine what my renovation was going to be. I came up with $8,500.

Because I was new to the area, I drove around the neighborhood and took the time to look at the closed sales (comparables) and make sure I was comparing similar homes in the same kind of neighborhoods. Also, I watched for any "For Sale" signs in the area, by either homeowners or Realtors. I called about similar homes and inquired about condition and pricing. (Another good tip when you're entering a market that you're not familiar with is to research sales in the neighborhood to see which of those were sold by investors and which by homeowners. A good way to tell if a sale was by an investor is if the name of the seller or owner is under a company name. You can also research what price that investor paid for that property in that area. After doing good research on this, you should be able to detect a trend. Not every investor buys the property at the same price, but it will help you get a feel for what other investors are buying in that area.)

I took a little extra time to make sure I established my market value, which in this case was $85,000. I also determined the renovation cost to be $8,500. I now took 70% of $85,000, which is $59,500, I subtracted $8,500 in renovations, and I subtracted $10,000 for closing costs and holding time, which left me with a maximum purchase price of $41,000. Since their asking price was only $30,000, there was no reason for me not to purchase the property.

I followed up with a Realtor who was listing the property for the seller. The Realtor told me that the seller was motivated to sell it at the same time the seller listed it, at a price that would sell quickly; therefore, he was not that negotiable. Remember, I determined that I could pay as much as $41,000. I chose to go ahead and give the seller the full asking price of $30,000 and lock up the property as soon as possible. Again: The key to getting good deals in this business is to act swiftly. Plenty of people are willing to pay what you are—or even more than the asking price. He who acts the fastest and puts it under contract will get the property first. Someone may want to pay more than I, but he may take longer to get to the seller. That can cost him the deal. So, based on my experience, I just went ahead and gave him the full asking price. Only six hours into my trip, I already had a fully executed contract to purchase an investment property. This is a perfect example of the urgency and aggressiveness that I so much advocate in this book.

Since I bought the property at such a good price, getting financing was not a challenge. I ended up borrowing $45,000 toward the property. The title company took approximately three weeks to do the closing and hand me my title insurance. We had a few handymen give us quotes, and we took the cheapest one, which was $7,000. Remember, I had estimated the renovation to be $8,500. Estimates should always be higher than the projected actual cost.

The renovation started shortly after the closing. We were faced with a few challenges. This home had a nice yard and lot, but the home wasn't very big, and the roof had a little bit of a dip in the back portion of the home. So when you entered the home, you had a bedroom on the left, and a bedroom on the right, then you walked through the living room, and in the rear you had a kitchen on one side and a bathroom on the other. We did not have the greatest floor plan, since both bedrooms were in the front part of the house, and in the back part of the home you had the kitchen and the bathroom. The biggest challenge in marketing this house was that the ceiling in the back part of the home was not as high as the front part of the home. And it's not that the home was defective; it was just the way it was built. It was very hard to elevate the second part of the home because you would have to re-do the roof and change a lot of the foundational part of the home, which would destroy any possible profit on this home. So making those adjustments was not an option. Despite renovating the home with a new kitchen, new bathroom, new carpet, paint inside and out, and bringing the property to market condition, I was still dealing with the ceiling drop in the second part of the home.

Since the house had floor plan issues and ceiling height issues, I chose not to market this home until it was completely renovated. I was worried about some major challenges that come with selling a home, and I did not want show the property unfinished. Whenever someone walked through, I wanted the home to look as good as possible to try to compensate for the visible structural deficiencies.

It took one month to rehab the home, and then I started my marketing campaign. I put a homemade sign in front of the property stating that the seller would help with closing costs and that the mortgage would be $700 a month, depending on credit and interest rate. To rent this home would cost the same amount of money or more. I tried to get the sign to interest as many people as possible. There are plenty of programs out there that, depending on the buyer's credit, lend up to 95% of the purchase price, and allow the seller to contribute up to 6% toward the buyer's closing costs. This means to me, as a seller, if my property is worth $85,000, the buyer will end up contributing 6% of the closing cost, or $5,100, which means I'm really selling it for approximately $80,000. I don't mind selling at a discount if I can find a buyer fast. Here, I believed that giving a buyer great terms and making it easier for someone to buy would overcome the challenges that I had in the odd floor plan.

The first calls I got were from next-door neighbors interested in the home for a family member. I had met the neighbors during my inspection of the ongoing renovations; I had introduced myself, and later they showed up on the doorstep. Unfortunately, once they went into the home they were a bit disappointed with the floor plan and chose to move on. I also put an ad in the paper that said the same thing as my sign. I received a slew of calls. A gentleman called and expressed interest. He soon went to see the home and agreed to give me a deposit and write up a contract. I was excited that I had found a buyer. But when he came back with his wife and she went through the home, she didn't like it, and I gave them their money back and voided the contract. Ah, well.

So, here I was going through myriad buyers, trying to find someone, anyone. But I still believed in the decision that I had made and I never lost faith in my initial gut feeling that there was *someone* out there for this property.

Within days, I got another call. This person was interested in the house and at that moment was living with family members. I asked the usual questions of my potential buyer, such as, What do you do for work? How's your credit? Have you owned properties before? Where do you live now? Where are you originally from? And, based on this information, I offered a plan that could make both of us happy—that's the key to selling.

The buyer loved the home and was unhappy with his present living situation. Not every deal is the same so I use discretion to make adjustments in order to secure buyers for properties. I'll do this all the time, but sometimes you need to improvise. I suggested to him that he rent the property while we were doing the paperwork. Of course I would prequalify him first, and he would use my mortgage broker. Depending on that information, I would allow him to move in and rent it on a month-to-month basis until the loan was completed. I told him that he could start living there right now, if he qualified, and start paying rent until the loan was done. He wouldn't have to move again; he had enough to worry about, and I would make things easier for him. In fact, I even offered a low rent of only $550. That was my mortgage, and since I would be paying a mortgage regardless, why not have somebody there covering it until I have a sale?

Since I was helping him with closing costs and giving him a discount on the rent, these benefits certainly offset an imperfect floor plan. He would have to be crazy to say no. As you may have guessed, he liked everything I had to say, so we signed a month-to-month lease. When he was prequalified with my mortgage broker, he gave me the first month's rent and moved in. This reinforced my original thought that there was definitely someone out there who would love these terms. I got absolutely no resistance with the asking price of $85,000.

Since my mortgage broker was doing the loan, I felt very comfortable that things would move forward. Hopefully, I would have a sale and closing within the next 45 days. The loan took closer to 65 days, which was not the end of the world for me as I was covering my mortgage with his rent. Most of the time, mortgages take longer to close than the actual contract date because so many things have to come together and so many people have to come together; it's just part of the business. If things take longer than the contract, just try to find out what's happening and what remains to be done. You need to work with everybody around you and create a team atmosphere to get it done. We had a closing and sold the property.

It took me eight months from the day I purchased the property to sell it and actually get paid. I was into the property for $45,000. I took in $75,000, after my seller's contribution toward the buyer's closing costs and my own closing costs, netting a profit of $30,000.

My ability to recognize deals, analyze deals, and act quickly allowed me to get this put together in a very short time. As long as I properly plan and execute, I will consistently profit. This business is about getting as many income streams going as consistently as you can, to consistently be able to profit. That translates into a constant cash flow and income stream. That constant income stream is one of the biggest challenges that investors face. Because real estate takes time and things don't usually happen when you expect them to, you need to have as much going on and as many seeds planted as you can handle. And being aggressive in marketing and acquisitions is what ties it all together. From the time I learned how to purchase real estate on a regular basis, I have maintained a substantial inventory—from 30 properties to 50 properties available for sale—at all times. This translates into constant cash flow.

Here are some lessons from this transaction:

Once you learn this business, you can take it with you anywhere you go

Try to put the property under contract even if you don't see it

As long as you communicate with the seller and have contingency clauses in the contract or letter of intent.

When you show a property to a potential buyer, try to have all the decision-makers present

Finally, as promised, here is a lesson in how to use knowledge of industry terms to your profitable advantage

Every real estate investor should learn the key industry terms used in marketing and advertising properties for sale. These terms are in classified ads and in MLS customized searches where you can search with keywords. The presence of these terms does not guarantee you will find a bargain, but you can use them to minimize your search and save time. This method allowed me to quickly qualify and narrow down a big list to a smaller one, more focused on prospective properties that I might then make offers on. Here are a few sample terms:

Handyman Special: Almost certainly this will need some kind of work, from minor cosmetic work to full-fledged renovations.

As Is: Usually indicates that the property is in some kind of disrepair, but the seller will not or cannot take the time to do the work before the sale.

REO: Real Estate Owned by banks or lending institutions

Corporately Owned: Any property that is owned by companies, not individual names.

Divorce: Self-explanatory

Estate: Properties that must be sold after the death of an owner

Must Sell: Obviously, this owner wants to sell fast (or wants you to think this is a real bargain, true or not)

Needs TLC: Tender Loving Care, or, may be real rough

Fixer-Upper: See Handyman Special

You're looking for a distress sale, which means the seller is out of town, is a bank, or simply must sell, as is, etc. Train yourself as an investor to look at specific clues. I like to see how long the property has been on the market and price changes, if any. I mainly look at the remarks on the property. Most properties for sale are pretty much priced at market value, and our goal as investors is to find properties below market so we can turn a profit. Sometimes properties are already priced at a good deal, and sometimes they're priced at not such a great number, but you can negotiate the price. You don't know unless you try if a person is willing to negotiate a great discount. You never know what a seller's motivation is unless you try!

Case Study Ten

Tax Deed with Someone Else's Money

The next deal was a purchase of a tax deed property. As discussed earlier, tax deeds are sold through the local courthouse in a process similar to a foreclosure auction. When homeowners don't pay their real estate taxes, cities auction off delinquent tax debts using what is called a "tax certificate." If a property owner, for example, owes back taxes of $3,000 on a piece of real estate, the city will use a tax deed sale to collect that money. The city auctions off that tax bill to individuals who want a handsome return on their money. The auction starts at an 18% interest rate and works its way down to a final bid of whatever minimum rate that tax deed investor is willing to accept as a return on his or her money. Individual investors, of course, receive that agreed-upon interest rate as their rate of return, just like all of us might receive a particular rate of return on a savings account or a bond we invest in. After several years of selling tax certificates on the same property, the county will take the property from the homeowner through a certain protocol. In turn, any loans or rights and ownership to the property are forfeited, and the county becomes the legal owner. Therefore, any mortgages, ownerships, and prior deed transfers to any individuals or companies are all null and void. The county is the new owner, free and clear of any deed or mortgage encumbrances, with one exception.

Any government liens, violations, or fees associated with government debts remain attached to the subject property. This is quite different from a foreclosure sale, where all existing liens are removed from the property upon conclusion of the foreclosure sale. In a tax deed sale, all fines continue to accrue, and all violations remain attached to the property. (You may recall a past investment in which I purchased a property from an investor who in turn had purchased it through a tax deed sale.)

With 99.9% of transacted properties, buyers purchase title insurance. Recall that title insurance is an insurance policy that protects the proper ownership of a property, and ensures that no one from the past can claim that your property belongs to him or that he has any rights to your property. And if such a person does come forward in the future with such claims that turn out to be legitimate, you have an insurance policy that will protect you against any such losses. With tax deed sales, the property is *not* insurable with title insurance. You must go through that "quiet title action" to be able to properly acquire title insurance. That can take anywhere from 90 days to a year depending on the complexity of the case, after which time you can insure and protect yourself from any risks associated with proper ownership. And, most importantly, you can sell the property. Most people need to be able to purchase title insurance to buy a piece of real estate. At any rate, most buyers need a mortgage, and any mortgage company will require free and clear title as well as a title insurance policy to fund the deal. The quiet title action announces to the world that any persons who may have an interest in this particular property need to come forward within a specified time and show reason why the property may belong to them. Usually, the county has done its due diligence, and published all required notices associated with physically taking a property back.

So, for us as real estate investors, tax deeds are just another way to purchase properties. You must understand that education in this subject area is necessary for every step in the process.

Tax deeds are sophisticated because you cannot depend upon a title company to provide you with free and clear title before you purchase the property and you must conduct the research without their help. Another challenge lies in the fact that you must purchase and pay for the property the same day you submit the winning bid, though as you may imagine, this speedy process eliminates many competitors. You also need to have a municipal and liens search done in advance just to know what you are inheriting. Once you're the owner, you are inheriting all the problems and violations that exist on the property. Tax deeds sales are, however, listed a few weeks before the actual sale. So you have some time to look at the properties for sale and make sure you know what you're looking at. Make sure you are comfortable with this process before you proceed.

So, with so many challenges, why would I want to acquire real estate this way? As they say in finance class, the higher the risk, the higher the return. But in real estate, risk is offset by knowledge, and that comes with research and doing your homework in advance. So if I'm taking on all these challenges, you can bet that I'm looking to purchase tax deeds at a much more significant market discount than I would if I purchased the property from a conventional seller offering far less uncertainty.

As I looked at the list that was published by the county, I had two weeks to prepare my research before their sale date. Since this way of acquiring real estate requires cash, I don't necessarily go to the sale every single time the auction takes place. There usually aren't a significant number of properties for sale at any one tax auction. For this particular week, I found 12 properties on the list, and most of them, I would say perhaps eight properties, were empty lots.

Now keep in mind why these properties ended up for sale like this in the first place. These property owners couldn't pay their real estate taxes for quite a number of years, to the point where they lost the property to the city. Usually, in a conventional ownership, there is some kind of mortgage on the property, and the lender will always protect its investment (which is the subject property). The lender makes you sign a note in which you personally guarantee the loan, but a lien is also placed on the property as a first mortgage, or even a second mortgage. In the event that you don't pay your note, the mortgage company will place a derogatory notice on your credit and may eventually take the property back to recover the company's initial investment. If you read the actual mortgage that you sign, it states in the note that a borrower must maintain and keep up his or her taxes and insurance, among other things. If you don't, the mortgage company will pay these costs for you and then bill them on a monthly basis. If you don't pay your monthly payments, the mortgage company will eventually pursue a foreclosure, and you will lose your property. Why am I telling you this? Because, generally, if there is a mortgage on a property, the bank won't let the tax bill remain delinquent for a long period of time (unless the bank has a major organizational malfunction within the company). So, most of the properties sold through tax deeds are done due to absentee owners who abandoned their property or seriously mismanaged it, and most properties carry no mortgages. Many are abandoned empty lots. About 30% of the offered deals are actual homes, with the unimproved lots making up 70% of the sales. Even though I have purchased and sold a few lots through this source, I mainly look for improved properties to renovate and sell.

So I noticed 12 properties for sale: three single-family homes, one duplex, and eight lots. My job at this point was to perform sufficient research to ensure that I was certain of the status of whatever I might be buying. As I drove to the first three houses, I found that they were all single-family homes, two occupied and the other abandoned. When I visit this type of property, I strive to speak with the current tenant to find out if the tenant is a renter or owner and how long he or she has been living in the home. You see, the county will give the current owners the opportunity to pay off their tax bills on the last day and cancel the pending sale. Many people leave everything to the last minute, even something as important as the possibility of losing a $150,000 property for a $10,000 tax bill that has accumulated over several years. So a certain percentage of the sales will get canceled due to this option of paying the outstanding balance at the last second.

So I returned home to analyze the properties. The tenants of the first single-family homes I looked at happened to be the owners, and they told me they were planning to pay off their tax bill before the sale. I couldn't be sure if they were going to do it, but I chose not to waste any time and tried to focus my energy on what I thought I might be able to purchase.

So I chose to concentrate on the third single-family home and an abandoned duplex. Going back to the drawing board, I pulled out the tax roll and comparables for the single-family home, which was a three-bedroom, two-bath, and the duplex, which had a two-bedroom, one-bath on one side and a two-bedroom, one-bath on the other. My research indicated that the single-family home was valued at $175,000.

The duplex was valued at $210,000. When I physically looked at these properties, I had to be even more careful because of the amount of time the properties had been abandoned. The disrepair was greatly due to the amount of time that these properties were vacant.

The single-family home had a very bad roof. In fact, many months of rain had damaged the entire abandoned structure. Due to this water damage, the repair was too great to undertake, in my opinion. So I decided not to pursue the single-family home and concentrate on the duplex, which was in much better shape.

Once I chose the property I wanted to purchase, I called a title company that I use regularly, and for a nominal fee, they did a quick search on the property. This search would help give me an idea of any liens, violations, and monies owed to the city over the years. Regardless of the money owed, the price is somewhat negotiable with the city. But I still had to make sure that I was prepared to invest some capital on top of the purchase of the property and renovation costs.

Here is where this gets a bit tricky, though with proper research you can be prepared for any uncertainty. Once I got lien searches and municipal searches from my title company, I was better able to picture what kind of things I would have to deal with. Here, I found an unsafe structure case pending against the duplex. (This means that the property has been abandoned and deemed unsafe. From the city's point of view, if the property is not brought to code and secured within a reasonable amount of time, the city would move forward in an attempt to demolish the property. At this point, the property was on its way to be demolished.)

As a potential new owner, I can arrange a meeting with city officials and the inspector in charge of the property and express my interest in purchasing the property and my desire to bring the property up to code and to market condition. Having this meeting would allow me to determine if I would get the city's cooperation. This is to the benefit of the city, as well; not only would I improve the neighborhood, but I would also maintain the property, which would generate future real estate taxes for the city. This would be a win-win, and it is just a matter of communicating, working with the city, and staying well organized with the timelines. This property was in a middle- to lower-income-type neighborhood, which left this property in a vulnerable situation to constant break-ins.

So having the report from my title company, which cost me only $70 for the search, I arranged a meeting to meet with the inspector in charge of the property. During meetings like this, not only do I hope to get a time frame to repair the property, but I also try to negotiate some of the existing liens that are outstanding on the property. I have found that if I exercise proper diligence and am prepared and organized and ready to do all I can to get a property back on the tax rolls, city officials are usually very reasonable.

When I met with the city inspector, I expressed my interest in the property and told the inspector that I wanted to be sure that the city was willing to cooperate with me and give me the time to pull the necessary permits and do the work to bring the home back to market condition. I inquired about the current monetary fines. The property had outstanding fines in the amount of $17,000, for which the city agreed to accept $5,500. We also had a second fine for $6,300, for which they were willing to accept $2,300. These old fines would leave me with an additional cost of $7,800. Of course, I still had an outstanding unsafe structure case that needed to be resolved. The official told me that I would have to pull all the necessary permits and close out the case within a specified time. I would have 60 days to pull my first permits from date of ownership. This was all the information I needed, and now I felt a bit more certain about moving forward toward acquiring this property.

(Before we move on with this case, let me give you a bit of understanding and background on how monetary fines accumulate. When a violation exists, the city allows a certain amount of time for an individual to make repairs; if the owner fails to do so, the city starts assessing fines. For every fine and violation that exists, the city gives the property owner the right to express his or her side of the story at a hearing—be sure to observe some of these hearings in your area—and board members may then give extensions of deadlines, discount fines, or erase the fines altogether. In the end, some of these fines are enormous, hundreds of thousands of dollars, after racking up at a rate of $100 a day for years. Realistically, though, the fines can be negotiated down substantially.)

So back to my deal. The county was asking $28,000 for this property. That didn't mean that this was my purchase price; this was the cost of all of the taxes that were owed over the years, with late fees and interest accumulating through the tax certificate. The county was just looking to get its money back. Remember: This was an open auction, so many people would be bidding. The final sales price would depend upon the number of people bidding and how savvy they were. I am not sure how many people did the amount of due diligence that I did, but I promise you, there were not many. Knowing the physical condition of the property, knowing the city's position and the cooperation that the officials are willing to provide, knowing every detail possible, would assure me the greatest likelihood of bidding success and success in the long run if I did buy the property for investment.

The auction was three days away, and I summarized the figures: the property was worth $210,000. It would cost me $7,800 to pay off the city liens. I would also have to spend $3,500 on an attorney for the quiet title action to be able to sell the property. The city was asking $28,000, but unlike many buys where the purchase price is constant, in this case the purchase price could change by the second. I had concluded that the property needed $35,000 in work. Since that was a lot of work and I had some time, I decided to get back with my contractor and really nail down my renovation costs.

The property was in a great location right on the main street. When a home is on a high-traffic street, many buyers shy from it, but I don't. You've undoubtedly noticed by now that I try to sell most of my properties at a discount for a quick sale and a fast profit. Therefore, I embrace high-traffic visibility. If I have a property that is selling at a great price, the more people who see it, the better chance I have of selling. So the location of the property was a big positive in my book. The home needed a *lot* of work: new roof, new windows, new kitchen, new bathroom, re-wiring of the electrical system, and the usual cosmetic work. (But the house had solid floors, solid walls, and a rolled concrete base, which was key.) Since we were dealing with the whims of the city, I had to take under consideration possible additional costs that they might pop up with. We also had to pay an engineer and architect to properly pull permits. These professional costs alone, depending on the size of the project, can be extremely costly; in my case, it would cost $7,500 for the 2,000-square-foot duplex. So after meeting with a contractor and discussing all the permit fees and any other professionals who would be involved, I confirmed that $35,000 was a sufficient estimate.

Let's discuss financing again for just a moment. Since you have to come up with the money the same day of the tax auction, you need to arrange financing before you go. Unlike a conventional deal, where you can put the property under contract and then have 30 days to get everything lined up, you'll have no such luxury here. As it turned out, I had an investor friend with an equity line of credit on his home. (Remember, as you start showing success, people gravitate toward you to be part of that success. And when you know what to do in real estate and how to make money, you can put people's money to work. I am a big fan of partnerships in this business.)

So, my friend had a home equity line of credit for $150,000 and wanted to participate. With his home credit line, he could pull as much or as little of the line as he wished, and at good rates. In exchange for me finding the deal and putting everything together, my investor friend would access a portion of his equity line to finance the deal.

When you go into auctions, you need to have a maximum number in mind that you are going to bid. So there I was, crunching numbers and trying to determine what was the most I was willing to pay. The market value was $210,000. Assuming my usual 70% of that, which in this case was $147,000, and subtracting $35,000 in renovations and $3,500 in attorney's fees for the quiet title action left me at $108,500. I further subtracted the $7,800 for fines to pay the city and needed to take under consideration financing expenses and holding time. We had in mind a holding time of one year, because of the long rehab and the quiet title action. Not knowing what our actual purchase price was going to be yet, we calculated an extra $15,000 in holding time and then subtracted 20% for incidentals. I was left with a purchase price of a maximum of $68,000. That amount would be the most I would be willing to pay for this property. By action time, I had done all I could, and it was time to go bidding.

I got to the county courthouse at 9:00 in the morning. It was a hectic day; the courthouse crowded with people. My house was third on the list for sale, so I sat and observed the first two auctions. By the time my property was coming up, I had the butterflies. The bidding started at the $28,000 asking price. I kept quiet while a few people started to bid. The home quickly went to $30,000 and then up to $38,000. Soon it reached $42,000. At this point, I had yet to say one word. There were fewer bidders as the price started to escalate.

The bidding went to $45,000, and at this point there were only three bidders competing. Now I got into the bidding war. I bid $47,000. One guy fell off, and it came down to me and another gentleman. He offered $48,000, and I came up to $52,000. He said $53,000, and I said $56,000. Note he was making small incremental increases while I was making much larger increments in hopes of making a statement that I would not be denied. I think my strategy worked. He noticed that I was making much bigger leaps, which meant it would cost him much more money to purchase the property than he probably had hoped. He soon backed off, and I won the bid for $56,000—$12,000 below my maximum offer. I went to the bank, got a cashier's check for $56,000, and brought it back to the county in exchange for the tax deeds. I was now the owner of a very ugly, very run-down duplex. Sounds exciting, doesn't it?

Now there was a lot of work to do. I immediately gave the attorney a copy of the tax deeds and let him get to work and clear up the title so I could buy title insurance and be in the position to sell or refinance this property. At the same time, I started my renovation process.

It took three months before the architectural plans, engineering reports, and permits were approved by the city, and we could start the renovation work. When doing this much extensive work, sometimes getting all the approvals takes longer than the work itself!

So what now? I put my sales hat on!

Since this property was on a major street with excellent exposure, I knew a lot of people had their eyes on it. Therefore, I prepped my contractor and his employees to keep an eye out for anyone who expressed interest in the property while they were working. Neighbors are a great source of buyers; the majority of the time, they have friends or family members hoping to move close to them. Given that this particular property had been abandoned for so long, any new activity would bring a positive spin to neighbors and the neighborhood. As I had predicted, shortly after the renovation started, an older lady approached my contractor.

The next-door neighbor was interested in buying the property for her cousin. She had had her eye on the property for a long time. Now, she was extremely excited that somebody had bought it and started the improvements. Having the property vacant and in disarray had put some strain on her property values, and her nerves. The constant break-ins at the subject property and the lack of maintenance and upkeep were something she had been dealing with for several years.

So you can imagine her reaction when this eyesore, derelict property was being brought up to code. This particular next-door neighbor had expressed her interest to my contractor, and he, being well trained to handle this, connected me with her.

I asked her, "Is it for you or someone else?"

"My cousin," she said.

"Is your cousin renting now?"

"Yes," she said.

She did not know how much her cousin was paying in rent, though, so she gave me his phone number.

After speaking to the potential new buyer, I told him that I was in the middle of total renovation, and it would take six months before I could sell him the property. He was fine with that, as he still had some lease obligation at his current rental. He really liked the location, as well as the fact that he'd be living next to a family member.

As an investor, I sorely wanted a buyer before my renovation and quiet title action were completed. So my objective with this buyer was to try to get a contract and deposit with the future closing date of six months. Being an aggressive closer is important. What do I mean by this? Most investors would have said, "Call me in six months." Maybe they would take a name and a phone number, then lose it and never follow up. Not me. I did my best to try to secure the sale of this property even before I was even legally able to sell it. I told my potential buyer the property was worth $210,000, but I would be willing to sell it to him for $180,000 as long as I could write up the contract and get a deposit that day. I also connected him with a mortgage broker I work with. He was soon prequalified and prepared to move forward. The buyer said he liked what I had to say and appreciated my honesty. I added to the contract an addendum that stated that the property had to be free and clear from any liens and violations and everything would be subject to a final report from the city stating that all necessary work had been completed to code. My buyer gave me a $2,000 deposit, and I had six months to finish everything.

So now it was up to my contractor and me to stay organized and work as diligently as possible to finalize this project. Four months into the renovation process, the city requested additional electrical permits—something we were not expecting, but we just had to go with any requests. Later, this would turn out to cost some time and money. As we were getting closer to the six-month deadline, most of the work had been done, and the title was finished. We were just doing minor adjustments and tasks that the city was requesting. The title company finished all the proper searches that they needed to do and they were ready to go, but the city released everything except for the electrical violation.

I was getting a lot of resistance from the city even though I had proved more than willing and able to do what I had been called upon to do. Some things are out of your hands, but you try to control as much as you can, especially when you're dealing with the government, which can be a bit slow. But my buyer was also ready, willing, and able, and I wanted to do what I could to close.

Here is what I did (and this is the type of creative and diligent strategy to keep in mind when you must get a deal closed).

I called the title company and asked if we could hold some money in escrow and give the seller a time frame to close out this violation so we could still complete the deal. Few investors have enough patience, or vision, or knowledge, so they shoot themselves in the foot time after time. I was into the property for about $110,000 at this point, so even if I received only $170,000 (having a title hold-back of $10,000, which I will get back at a future date anyway) I would make $60,000, get the property off my books, stop making mortgage payments, and get an additional $10,000 a few months down the road. It was the right play for this situation. Make some money now and make a little bit more later, but get it off the books. And that is exactly what I did. Two months later, I made a cool profit of $70,000; I split this with my investor friend 50/50, which still netted me $35,000 in profit.

Here are some lessons from this transaction:

Make sure you maximize all acquisition possibilities

Network with your contractor and his employees to find buyers among neighbors and their friends or families

Remember, "real estate is gambling, but gambling with knowledge"

Do as much homework as you can before you buy anything. Have the foresight to see down the road; even if your home is not ready for sale now, your objective is to sell, to try to find a buyer with a future closing date, even if it means giving a small discount to lock in the future, for it will give you peace of mind.

Get it off your books

If you have a closing schedule, try to close even if it means waiting for some of your money.

You want view aerial photos of the subject property

In order to determine the proper dimensions and lot lines. The reason I tell you this is that I once ran into a tricky situation, when trying to buy a lot, where if it hadn't been for my due diligence and savvy, I would have been in a "lot" of trouble. When I went to visit this lot, I spotted a home that seemed much bigger than the dimensions of the lot that was for sale! After doing some research, I found that the county was selling just a small strip of lot that was part of *another lot* that somebody was living on. If I had chosen to go ahead and purchase this, it would have been impossible to sell it. It would have been money thrown out the window. I had another incident where I was trying to buy a lot and soon learned, through physical research and viewing aerial photos, that the lot is what they call "land-locked," which means that the parcel was behind another parcel that was facing the street. I would have to get an easement (allowing me to carve out a driveway to my property) from the city and the other lot owner to be able to access the lot. So use Google or other aerial or satellite photo services before you buy. It may sound like work, but just think how you'll feel if you purchase a lot that you can't legally access!

Case Study Eleven

How I Made $39,000 by Spotting a "For Sale" Sign

Purchasing a "For Sale by Owner" property is another good way to buy. By now, I'm sure you've noticed my tenacity and sense of urgency when putting together a deal. It never stops in any aspect of this business. Don't be a secret agent; you need to constantly promote yourself.

Recently, I went to a few real estate seminars. The first thing I noticed was that new investors were promoting themselves as real estate investors. Even if they had never purchased a property before, they want to tell the whole world they buy houses. The first thing that they are taught, in various seminars and books, is to tell the whole world what you do. This is very good advice.

One time I had a property that was being renovated, and being responsible and always checking up on things, I drove by to see how it was going. Why? Once you focus on a neighborhood or "farm" an area, you become familiar with the market value and the types of homes. Making decisions on properties in an area you are familiar with becomes easier and faster. So as I was driving to my property, I saw a "For Sale by Owner" sign on one of the properties. I called while I was in front of the property. A lady answered the phone. I asked her many questions, including some about the number of bedrooms and baths. She politely answered my questions and told me (this is where it gets interesting) that it was a four-bedroom, two-bath home that had been converted into a rooming house. This meant that, in order to maximize her rent, she had turned it into six separate bedrooms, with two common bathrooms. She did not live in the property, but she lived close by.

I looked around the property. It had a very nice lot, and the property was in moderate shape. I asked her how she collected her rents and managed the property. She told me that one of the tenants was living for free, and he was collecting the rent for her and looking out for the property. As she lived in the area, she was happy to come right over and show me the property.

While she was on her way to meet me, I started to crunch some numbers. Since I had similar properties in the area, I knew the property was worth somewhere around $180,000. From the outside, I initially thought the property needed very little work, but when she showed up and we stepped inside, I noticed that the interior needed more work than I thought. The bathrooms needed upgrading. The interior needed paint and new carpeting. I estimated it to be about $7,000 worth of work. I asked the owner how much she was asking. To my surprise, she was asking only $100,000. So far, so good!

Part of the advantage of using a Realtor when selling a property is it gives you some education on the market and an understanding of what is available. Many sellers try to save money to the point that they either under-price or over-price their property. New investors should love Realtors. They have local knowledge of the market, and with the Internet and other technologies Realtors can easily communicate that information with buyers and sellers. So many sellers who try sell on their own may not have the proper information to make the right decision on the pricing of their property.

Now in this case, the seller had no mortgage on the property. I found this out later when I went back into my office and researched the tax roll. She was basically tired of managing the property and just wanted to get out. Real estate is a great business, but being a property manager is quite a bit of work. It sounds fantastic, and there are a lot of positive sides to being a landlord. But contrary to popular opinion, it is a constant on-call job that can wear anybody out. The good news is "property management." Let them do all the work for you. As we discussed earlier, property management companies will alleviate the daily stress of being a landlord.

After speaking to the lady and looking around the property,

I decided to jump on this opportunity before the word got out, and it would no longer be available. It is very important for you to understand and to keep in mind that I always keep blank contracts, usually at least six of them, as well as leases, in my car, all the time. I refer to this as my cash register. If you worked at a convenience store, you must have the cash register in order to take somebody's money in exchange for goods. Real estate works the same way. A contract or a lease is what enables a transaction. So I make it a point to always have these documents in my possession. Since you should always be out there looking to put deals together, you need to be prepared and put yourself in position to legally bid on a property.

I told the seller that I owned properties in the area already and was an investor. I had a contract on me, and I was willing to write it up, right now. I went to my car, got two contracts out (since she didn't have a copy machine, I would fill out two contracts—one for me and one for her). I offered her $90,000, and being prepared and as organized went a long way with the seller. The fact that I had a contract on me and was ready to write it up really made a difference. She accepted my offer. I wrote up a contract on the spot, took her information, gave her my information, and went home. This type of transaction happens all the time to those who are prepared to take advantage of opportunity.

When I got home, I pulled the tax roll, only to confirm my initial estimates of the $180,000 market value. As far as the rooming house was concerned, I figured I would bring the property back to its original four-bedroom, two-bath structure. I did not feel comfortable having the property run as a rooming house since it wasn't set up that way. I could run into trouble with the city and be forced to bring the property back to its original structure, plus the management would be much more intense. I put a deposit on the property and faxed the seller a copy of the escrow the next day. To make your contract legal, consideration (money) must change hands. Since the price was within my allowed budget, I wanted to make sure I solidified my contract so I had no chance of losing my rights to the property. I also asked the seller if it was okay if I gave the tenants notice to move and find another place to live (since I had to eliminate two bedrooms).

Bringing back the property to a four-bedroom two-bath was not a complicated task, since all we had to do was remove two walls. Using my formula, I determined the market value to be $180,000. I multiplied that by 70%, which comes to $126,000. I subtracted $10,000 for closing costs and holding time. I also subtracted an additional $10,000 for renovation. I came up with $106,000, which was the maximum I was willing to pay. I now had the property under contract for $90,000, $16,000 below the maximum. I felt great about this property and its potential. The seed was planted for future income. I needed to borrow $110,000. I didn't feel like that would be an issue since my numbers were very strong. At this point, I had developed a solid relationship with one particular lender. I was getting very little resistance with my loan requests. This helped me strengthen my buying power. I got the $110,000 loan approval, and now all I was waiting for was title to be completed and the closing scheduled. The closing was scheduled two weeks after my initial date of the contract.

My notice to the tenants to vacate was unsuccessful. Nobody moved out! I had to make a few decisions. At this point, I was the owner, and I had a mortgage to pay. I altered my plan of converting the property from four bedrooms and two baths to keeping it as a rooming house. Why? Well, this property had been around as a rooming house now for many years. The rooming house seemed to be working. I decided to leave it as a rooming house; if I had any issues in the future, I would just bring it back to a four-bedroom, two-bath house. But in the meantime, I benefited from the $2,000-a-month income, and I used this kind of income to justify a higher sales price to potential buyers. You see, if I was persistent in converting the home back to a house, I would have to go through six different evictions. This would cost me about $500 per eviction ($3,000) and two months of mortgage payments (an additional $2,000) so it would cost me $5,000 just to be able to start the renovation. Since the tenants did not want to move on their own, I simply informed them that they could stay and continue to pay rent. I felt that this decision was a much better one. To show good faith with the new tenants, I went ahead and changed all the appliances, changed the carpet, and painted inside and out. I continued my relationships with the tenants, and I maintained the manager who had been collecting and managing. I felt it was important to keep the existing gentleman on hand; this would save me time, and it would give me the best chance of collecting rent, since he had been in place and everyone was familiar with him.

Meanwhile, I was trying to sell this property to an investor. Originally, of course, my plan was to convert the property into a four-bedroom, two-bath house and sell it to a retail buyer. Since I was now keeping it as a rooming house, I could no longer sell it to someone who was going to live in the property. My focus was now to sell to an investor who wanted to keep it as a rental property. I could now try to promote the property as an income property and use the "income approach" for appraising the property. Since the property was generating $2,000 a month, I felt that the property was worth more than my initial estimate of $180,000. Since I was not very comfortable with the rooming house situation, I became very aggressive in promoting the property. Finding an investor-buyer was not easy. If you have a legal triplex, duplex, or four-plex, the floor plan and other details are very clear to a potential buyer. People don't understand rooming houses as clearly and get skeptical. So my salesman hat had to be on for this one.

Four months into the ownership of this property, something terrible happened. The current property manager became very ill and was hospitalized for a long period of time. Though of course hoping he would feel better, I had to continue my search for a buyer and now, also, a manager. For the first couple of months, I managed the property myself. It wasn't something I wanted to continue doing. It was taking a lot of my time that I could use for looking and selling more deals. I searched for another person in the neighborhood and luckily found somebody else to manage the property. Even though the rent income was $2,000 a month, I was only collecting $1,200 to $1,700 per month. Most of the tenants were either not home or paying in installments and constantly playing catch-up. Unfortunately, I had to continue working with them and do my best to collect as much as I could. That was a better option than trying to evict them; it would simply cost me too much money. But having a new manager improved the efficiency of collecting and communicating with the tenants, as I now had somebody present at all times.

Nine months into my holding time, I was still looking for a buyer. Sometimes when you are selling a property, the buyer needs to trust your opinion, your advice, and your game plan about the property and how it will make a profit for them.

During one of my usual monthly investor meetings, I met a buyer who was new in the business and looking to get started. I spent about 30 minutes speaking to him and giving him some knowledge and tidbits on how to do business. He liked what I had to say, and we had good chemistry. As I said earlier, people want to do business with you if they trust you. I felt strongly about the potential of this property for an investor. I, on the other hand, had too much going on, and it wasn't on my agenda to keep this particular property long-term. But, for an investor looking to get started, this was a great property with a great cash flow advantage.

After showing him all the advantages, he decided this was a property he wanted to pursue. I was asking $155,000. I decided I could leave a good spread for the buyer and still make a quick sale. I was still only into the property for $110,000 which left me a potential profit of $45,000. The buyer felt I was doing him a favor. Since this buyer was new, I connected him with the mortgage broker I was familiar with. This made the sale a bit stronger for me, knowing the mortgage was being worked on by someone who had proved himself. I took a $1,000 deposit and wrote the contract, and off we went.

As I indicated earlier, the income stream could alter the potential appraisal report. The value came in at $205,000, not the $180,000 I had initially thought. This extra $25,000 was a great benefit to this new investor/buyer.

When I sell a property to an investor in a wholesale environment, I like to do right by him or her. If I want him or her to come back and continue to buy from me, I want to make sure I treat the investor as best I can in hopes that he or she does well on the investment the investor purchases from me. Of course, I don't control much after the sale; it's up to the investor to make sure he or she manages it and runs the property correctly. But I do my best to give investors the strongest possible investment and keep my fingers crossed that things will work well for them. Selling them one property and never seeing them again is not the long-term strategy that I have in mind. I want repeat customers, and that comes only with good business. Fifty days after we signed the contract, we had a closing. I sold the property for $155,000 with $3,000 in closing costs; therefore, I netted $152,000. I was into the property for $113,000; I made a profit of $39,000.

Here are some lessons from this transaction:

You need to believe in what you do and believe in the business that you are in

Just think: I was driving around the neighborhood when I saw a "For Sale By Owner" sign. Using my people skills, my organizational skills, and my ability to be aggressive and take action, I put the property under contract on the spot and 11 months later made a profit of $39,000. I believe that when people work hard, unconditionally, and are consistent and persistent, something great will come to them. So when something goes your way but you don't know where it came from, remember: it came from the seeds planted when nothing was working, but you did not stop being consistent and persistent.

Case Study Twelve

A Quick Flip

As I was looking for more houses, I found a property through another investor. He had purchased the home for $80,000 and wanted to wholesale the property so he wouldn't have to close on it or renovate it. He was asking $90,000. As we discussed before, buying from wholesalers can often present excellent opportunities. There are a lot of investors who prefer to just flip properties, and I keep an active list of just such investors.

Once I found the lead, the first thing I did was look up and determine the comps, active sales, and possible available properties in the area. I determined the property to be worth $165,000. One of the reasons the property was offered at a low price was because it needed renovation. The owner didn't have the funds to fix it up, and so made the decision to flip it. Ask yourself: Why wouldn't the owner just sell it to someone who would live there? Most likely, the answer is that a retail buyer (someone who will live in the house) would not buy the house fast enough, if someone would buy it at all. Banks will not mortgage houses that are not in market condition, and most retail buyers don't have enough cash to purchase a property without a mortgage. There are some programs that will lend on non-renovated properties, but they are hard to find. Here, the seller was in distress and needed to sell fast. Time is money for house flippers.

So, the seller needed a fast closing; all I needed were the funds to close on the property. Over the years, you, as I have, will develop relationships with private lenders. You may recall, they give me the funds fast and with very little red tape. The interest rates are high and the loans short-term, but as long as I have enough profit potential, it is usually worth it.

I walked around the property (with my appraiser hat on) and looked at the marketability of the place (after donning my sales hat).

On this particular property, it seemed like someone had started to renovate but did not finish. There were open walls, but the kitchen and bathroom were in fine shape; they just needed fixtures. The electrical needed upgrading, and the house needed the usual cosmetic details such as paint inside, outside, and around the baseboards. The property needed general window cleaning and repairs to light fixtures.

I sent over a couple of contractors I had relationships with to work up bids. They both came back with an approximate renovation cost of $12,000. Now that I had established the renovation cost and market value, I knew what I was prepared to pay for the property. The price was $90,000, and renovation was $12,000. I also considered my holding cost for the mortgage. I determined the market value to be $165,000, and 70% of that is $115,500. So, I was in the clear, and ready and excited to get going.

I knew this was a good property, and I knew I would be buying it. I had to cement my intention for the property. Should I buy, fix, and sell? Should I buy, fix, and rent? Should I wholesale it (it is not unusual for a property to have multiple assignments)? Or should I buy, fix, and retail?

I decided to buy, fix, and retail. The area was nice, and the house had a lot of marketability, with especially good curb appeal. It was not a big home; just a two-bedroom one-bath, but it was on a nice-sized lot. I decided this was the best way to maximize my profit.

I picked an exit strategy and moved forward to close the property and to become the owner.

I closed the house, and renovation started. I like to renovate from the outside in. It is best to give the house a good look and start marketing the home ASAP. If I find a buyer before I put flooring or kitchen paint on the inside, I can give the new buyer the option to decide on the fixtures and colors.

I like using Realtors to sell my homes whenever possible, but as you've learned, I don't rely solely on them and the MLS (multilisting services) to sell my homes.

With this particular home, I put a sign in the front yard. I made one that looked very homemade and handwritten. Why? Because buyers tend to relate to "homegrown" rather than to a big company-type sign, because it smells more like a bargain. Naturally, it also depends upon the kind of neighborhood you are marketing to-use your discretion. Also, I spoke to some of the neighbors and told them I had a home that was under renovation, but I was already marketing it. As a usual part of my marketing, I like to help the buyers with closing costs. Lenders usually allow the seller to contribute 6% of the closing cost. This gives me an edge over other sellers. The neighbors are a good source of possible referrals. They almost always have family and friends whom they would love to have move next to them (maybe just friends, not family).

This property took me four weeks to renovate and about one month to find a buyer. I found the buyer through a next-door neighbor. I met with the lead, and the first things I wanted to make sure of was that he liked the home and everyone in the decision process was in agreement (remember, you don't want to sell to someone and then find out after wasting time that a spouse hates the place).

When I met with the buyer, I found out he did not have a mortgage broker, so I put him together with a reliable one. Even if the potential buyer has a mortgage broker, I will very carefully screen that broker, and if I don't feel comfortable, I will request he change to mine. I explain that this business can be a time waster, and I know that my broker is very respectful of his client's time. Remember, buyers ultimately do not want to waste time either.

The loan took about 45 days. I had purchased the property for $90,000. The closing costs and holding time were $10,000, and renovation was $12,000. I was into the property for $112,000. I sold it for $165,000. Then I paid $7,000 in closing costs on the sale, and my contribution toward the buyer's closing costs came to another $9,000. This left me a profit of $37,000. This deal took me about three months and approximately 40 hours of my time. Not bad!

Here are some lessons from this transaction:

Keep a Rolodex of investors and wholesalers
Network with all the local residents to find a buyer
Market while rehabbing

To learn more about all the skill sets involved in these types of transactions, visit my website at:

www.TheRoadToRealEstateWealth.com

Afterword:

Some Words to Help You Get Started

I am first and foremost an investor. Everything that I wrote in this book has come from study and experience. I first outlined what successful investors need to learn, and do, by describing all tasks necessary for success—those "hats" you will be wearing as you work. The case studies helped me illustrate and share some of the experience that I obtained over the years. Finally, the checklist and forms that follow are concrete tools for your business. Throughout the book, I have tried to prepare you for what is expected of you as a real estate investor.

Now, as a final note, I'd like to give you some tools to tackle the toughest opponents you'll face: Procrastination, Fear, and Doubt.

Goal Setting

The chances of accomplishing anything in life are greatly improved when a person writes his or her goals on a piece of paper, *with a deadline.* Many self-improvements books and success books insist on this, and I heartily agree with them. You see, a goal without a deadline is just a dream. Everyone who reads this book may have different objectives and, therefore, different goals. But everyone needs to have short-term goals, defined as your daily and weekly objectives, and stick to deadlines.

For example, my daily goal could be talking to one new person a day. And perhaps my weekly goals will be defined as making five offers a week. My monthly goals may be purchasing one property per month. (As my long-term goal, I may have total properties that I am trying to acquire within a one-year term.) If your goals are ambitious and you set high standards for yourself, you need to intensify your short-term goals. If you're looking to purchase more properties in a short period of time, you need to take more action and work harder than someone merely looking to diversify his or her income or acquire a few properties for retirement. The more specific, detailed, and clearer your goals, the better chance you have of being successful in achieving those goals. So, please, set those goals, be especially careful to stick to the short-term ones, and you will find your way on to great accomplishments—in every aspect of your life that you do so.

Before starting any new enterprise, big businesses spend hundreds of hours and thousands of dollars formulating a business plan. Yet, so many people go through their entire lives without a plan. Many climb the ladder of life only to find out that the ladder was leaning on the wrong wall. Do you believe that there are people out there who are efficiently ineffective? What I mean is that, typically, those who work the hardest physically usually will make less money than those who work effectively and efficiently.

Before starting any endeavor, you must first map out a clear and detailed strategy. As I mentioned to the point of trying your patience, TIME is our biggest asset. Ben Franklin said, "Time is the stuff of which life is made." You only get so many minutes of life, and the joke is you don't know how many minutes! That which is wasted is gone forever.

Many of you have full-time jobs and are looking to real estate as a way to break free from the rat race that is corporate America. Some of you may be successful business owners who want to find more time to spend with your families. The truth is, a real job may feel like prison with a paycheck. And when you own your own business you may sometimes wonder if, rather, it owns you.

Want to change things? You'll need to live the gospel that the more organized you are and the better you are at planning and setting specific goals and deadlines, the closer you'll be to achieving the financial freedom you are looking for.

Remember: Before getting out there and seeking your fortune, make certain you have in hand a solid business plan with specific, detailed goals and deadlines that you will diligently follow. Our time is a gift not to be wasted!

Taking Action

It's true. You can have all your plans and goals mapped out, but without action, nothing gets done. One of the secrets to being successful in this business is consistency and follow-through. These two can only be achieved through *action*. Sometimes I speak to new investors who always are "getting ready to get ready." Do you know what I tell them? Let your actions be your calling card. Make your actions speak so loud that no one need hear anything coming out of your mouth. Yes, just do it!

And help others take action. You have to follow up with people, and make sure they do what they're supposed to do. Nothing gets done until *you* make sure it gets done. If you properly and consistently follow up with Realtors, contractors, vendors, and anyone who helps put a deal together, this will help your entire business run with remarkable efficiency. Which means big profits.

Attacking Your Fears

One of the biggest obstacles that most people have when trying to accomplish something new and unknown is *fear*. The more knowledge you acquire and action you take, the closer you will get to overcoming your fears. Working hard is not the secret to success, but without hard work, you don't stand a chance. The only way to really conqueror fears is to attack them with action, in your business and personal life.

Several years back, I took a course to become a certified scuba diver. When I did my first ocean dive, I was a bit nervous about encountering barracudas. They're curious and intimidating fish that I heard some horror stories about, and I became a bit fixated on this unlikely danger. During my first ocean dive, I spotted a few barracudas at a distance, and I kept my eye on them. About two weeks later, I did my second ocean dive. I strapped on my tank, goggles, and weight belt. I took one step and dove right into the Atlantic Ocean.

As I was descending to a depth of 40 feet, my fears of

encountering barracudas haunted my thoughts. I looked to my right and spotted about four or five barracudas. When I turned to my left, I saw a school of more than 1,000 barracudas! I was terrified but held my position. My fear, really just fear of the unknown, started to fade. At this point, I had no choice but to see these curious fish as just that—curious. By diving right into my fears (so to speak), I realized it wasn't as bad as I had thought, and I got over it. In fact, every time I scuba dive I *look* for barracudas. If you have a fear of speaking to people, then start speaking to people. To achieve what we want in life, we need to overcome our weaknesses by attacking them with *action* by turning those fears to strengths.

Finale

Having financial freedom is one of the most incredible achievements that any individual can attain. You see, financial freedom means a lot of different things to a lot of different people. To me, financial freedom is not having to ask anybody for permission to take a vacation or to spend time with my family. It can mean having six Saturdays and one Sunday in any given week. It means spending time exercising, playing sports, reading, and doing anything that you want to do for you. It also means doing things during the time that everybody is working and streets are quiet.

The highway of success is never crowded, nor is the interstate busy at three o'clock in the morning. The fact is, when you go on vacation and spend $1,500 a night doing it, you won't have to deal with a crowd, and most likely will be treated like royalty. I tell you this not to brag but to convince you that such living is attainable and real—I started as an immigrant with nothing, and if I can do it, you can, too. To be able to achieve this lifestyle at such an early age against all odds is definitely proof that you don't have to come from money or be born into it or have a magic formula. You need to listen, as I have, and learn from other people's mistakes and experiences and then duplicate them. And with this book, I want to make it all that easier. Here's a question: What is the best way to walk through a minefield? I've asked this many times, and 90% of the time I did not get the response I sought. The answer is very simple: "Follow somebody." If you do, and he gets into trouble, you've learned just where not to step.

During my career, I've helped many people become successful in this business, and there's nothing more rewarding than to see someone change her life by breaking out of the rat race, achieving financial freedom, and strengthening her self-confidence. Success is a journey, not a destination, so you need to enjoy the climb and ask yourself every day before you go to bed: Did I learn something new today? If the answer is yes, you had a successful day.

Every morning in Africa when a lion wakes up, it knows it needs to outrun the slowest gazelle in order to survive. Every morning in Africa when a gazelle wakes up, it knows it needs to outrun the fastest lion in order to survive. The lesson: It doesn't matter if you are a lion or a gazelle, when that sun comes up you had better be running.

Work hard, work smart, learn all you can, be generous and fair, and good things will follow.

Part Three:
Tools and Forms

Through all my years of experience and completing hundreds of real estate deals, I have developed, through trial and error and experience, checklists and tools that help me manage my real estate investment business. The basic real estate forms such as purchase contracts, leases, and the like are available through various Realtor services providers, lawyers, title companies, local office supply stores, and the Internet. These forms are your basic fill-in-the-blank forms. They are neutral and fair and balanced; many of the forms here are custom designs that I have developed through trial and error and will help simplify and highlight significant details of different aspects of the business.

These will assist you to make offers more efficiently and will simplify the management and organization, with a checklist format, for your day-to-day duties.

This business is not a regular, nine-to-five job. The more you treat it like a real job, the better your chance of succeeding. These forms help me stay focused on the task at hand, and whenever I feel I'm getting sidetracked, I refer back to these forms to bring me back to the most important next step. This is how I stay productive. The checklists identify the key aspects of each area of a transaction.

To find these and other necessary forms, visit my website at www.TheRoadToRealEstateWealth.com.

Form: Buying Sources and Techniques

This form lists most of the ways to purchase real estate, and all the different wells that we spoke about earlier. One of the most important aspects of this business is to buy real estate. So having all the avenues to purchase up front will help you stay focused.

BUYING SOURCES & TECHNIQUES

A. Leads to buy properties
   1) Realtors
      a) Develop personal relationship with real estate brokers/salespeople to send you deals.
      b) Research brokers who specialize in distressed properties.
   2) MLS
      a) Once you develop relationships with licensed agents, make sure they update you with any new listings that come out in the MLS.
      b) Here is a good reason to have a license. This would save you time and allow you to do the searches yourself as well as offers. Also take back commissions.
   3) Banks (purchasing directly)
      a) Banks lists. Some banks choose to sell direct or have an internal department to sell their REOs.
      a) Search for services that provide list of foreclosures.
   4) Pre-foreclosures
      a) Use a foreclosure investor program to find leads.
      b) Contact banks directly for loan discounts that are in default.
   5) HUD
      a) Closed bids auction sales.
   6) VA
      a) Closed bids auction sales.
   7) Estates
      a) Find out when estates must sell (divorce/probate).
   8) Courthouse/Foreclosure sales/ Tax deed sales

   a) Buyer must develop relationships with people who work at the courthouse.
   b) Find out when all sales are going to take place.

9) Bankruptcy Court
   a) Develop relationships w/bankruptcy attorneys.
   b) Develop relationships w/bankruptcy trustees.
10) FSBOs (For sale by owners)
   a) Drive by neighborhoods; take "for sale by owner" numbers.
   b) Research the Internet "for sale by owner" sites for deals.
   c) Find all Internet FSBO sites.
11) Other investor lists
   a) Network with other investors.
   b) Visit real estate investment clubs.
12) Newspaper ads

Form: Process of Making Offers Most Efficiently

You are about to enter a very competitive market; therefore, time is always of the essence. I developed a form to keep on track and to be efficient and effective when making an offer. Investors who work fast and efficiently will get more offers accepted than those who drag their feet.

Process of making offers most efficiently

Note: Everything on this form must be done the same day.

1. Get leads
   - A. Buying sources and techniques.
   - B. All the ways there are to buy.
   - C. You generate leads to be able to make an offer on.

2. Review Lists
   - A. Look at address, price, key words, and agents.
   - B. Ways to screen and qualify the leads.
   - C. Call agent for availability.
   - D. Look at the locations you may be familiar with.
   - E. Look at the asking price.
   - F. Look at the remarks and description of the property that can tell you a lot about the property fast.

3. Appraisal Hat
   - A. Tax roll, your real estate agent, driving to property, calling for sales area. These are the ways to find out the real market value.
   - B. Do your homework and come up with a market value.

4. General Contractor Hat
   - A. Property condition, cost to bring property to market condition.
   - B. You need to determine renovation cost.

5. Note: The offer must be presented the same day, either verbally or in writing.
   - A. Time is of the essence.

6. Investor Hat
   A. Formula, decision time.
   B. Use the formula I have been teaching you.

Used to decide if you will make an offer on a prospective real estate investment. Goal is to complete tasks in a single day. Used to outline decision process and move faster than the competition.

Form: Letter of Intent

This helps an investor save time by testing the waters before making a formal offer. It also appears more credible than a verbal offer. This form is used as a synopsis of a contract and highlights only the important terms in a full contract. This form is used to get the ball rolling on an offer. Most contracts are long and very detail-oriented. You and your Realtor don't want to spend a lot of time writing a contract only to find out the offer was too low or rejected. It's much easier to write a one-page offer and start the negotiation process with a seller; this opens the communication line with the seller much faster and puts you a step closer to acceptance.

LETTER OF INTENT TO PURCHASE REAL ESTATE

Note: This is not a contract; once you have agreed with the terms, you must then follow up with a full contract.

FROM (Buyer) ____

Phone_______________

TO (Seller) ____

Phone_______________

This LETTER OF INTENT sets forth the basic terms and conditions upon which the Buyer agrees to purchase the property described herein.

This is a LETTER OF INTENT only. It does not create a legally binding obligation on the parties or their agents. This LETTER OF INTENT is subject to agreement between the parties upon a purchase and sale agreement containing the terms and conditions that the parties find agreeable.

PROPERTY ADDRESS: ____________________________________

____

____

LEGAL
DESCRIPTION:____

TERMS & CONDITIONS: Purchase Price:____________________
Cash Offer, "AS IS," Subject to Buyer's inspection
Proof of funds to close to be provided upon acceptance.
Deposit of $1000.00 will be made upon acceptance.

CLOSING shall take place on or before ________________________________.
A FORMAL PURCHASE AGREEMENT must be executed within 24 hours after acceptance of this letter.
EXPIRATION - This letter shall expire at ________PM on ________________, 20 unless previously accepted by the Seller.
AGREED/OFFERED: AGREED/
ACCEPTED:

____
BUYER DATE

____
SELLER DATE

____
SELLING AGENT

Form: Property Inspection Analysis

One of the variables you need to determine quickly in order to make a decision is the renovation cost (to bring the property to market condition). One of the most important Rolodexes you need to develop is your contractor and sub-contractor list. You need to develop your skills and increase your knowledge to the point that you can make a fast estimate of your costs; you won't always have a contactor to give you an estimate (as fast as you need). This is vital to your profit potential! You need to determine these costs on your own, eventually. Take your time with this topic. If you are not comfortable with determining the cost of renovation, use a contractor estimate. Make sure you get the estimates in writing, of course. Doing this may cost you a bit of extra time; you may even lose a deal or two. But don't despair; you need to be comfortable in this area. You need to be able to project a contractor's estimate. You want to avoid surprises. Some things will be out of your hands no matter how skilled you get at this. Spending time in home improvement centers and shadowing contractors will move you toward this goal. Develop a form or checklist that works for you, with a breakdown and a summary of where the property fits into this scheme after doing multiple rehabs. I am providing you the form that worked for me; you can start with that form and add to it as you see fit. If you focus on a specific neighborhood and style of home, you find yourself doing renovations that are modified to that specific demand.

PROPERTY INSPECTION ANALYSIS

Note: This form is another way to keep a quick track of rehab cost. You need to take your time and customize a form that is suitable to your market area and renovation standard.

PROPERTY INSPECTION REPORT

Property Adress:____

Curb Appeal: Good / Fair / Bad
Neighborhood: Good / Fair / Bad

Home Layout: Bed_____ Bath_____

Home: Attached / Detached

Structure: CBS / Frame

Carport / Garage

Additions / Conversions: ____

____

Landscaping:
Other ____________________

Roof:
Other _____________

Wood around Roof:
Other_______________

Meter: Yes No

INTERIOR

A/C: Units Central

Water Heater:

Appliances:

Kitchen:
Other________________

Bathrooms:
Other________________

Doors:
Other________________

Windows:
Other_______________

Carpet:
Other_______________

Tile / Vinyl:

Other_______________

Paint: Inside Outside

Other_______________

Switches, Outlets & Fixtures:
Other_______________

Electrical Work:

Other_______________

Total: ______________________

Form: Marketing Strategies

Marketing begins the moment you have a property under contract. This form will list all the ways that you might sell a property. You may not use every technique, but you can choose from the list those most likely to help you sell. You need to have all the sources that are available to you in your marketplace. Try to implement as many of the sales strategies as possible.

All the Ways to Sell:

RESIDENTIAL INVESTMENT SALES

A. *Newspaper ads*
   1) Analyze ads on a regular basis and look for key remarks.
   2) Run ads for properties that need to be sold.
   3) Place an ad for each section based on property address.
   4) Analyze previous leads from ads.

B. *MLS*
   1) Make sure all properties for sale are being marketed in the MLS for sale with a Realtor.
   2) Review the listing with your Realtor to check the progress.

C. *Tracking Offers*
   1) Set up files to track & report all offers: include date, amount, buyer, and buyer's contact info source (Other brokers, salesperson, MLS, ads, etc.).
   2) To follow up with potential contract for future deals.

D. *Fax Property List and Email Property List*
   1) Fax & email properties for sale to potential buyers and agents.
   2) Categorize potential buyers into specific areas and types of homes that they are interested in.
   3) Promote new properties as you put them under contract via email or fax.
   4) Use the power of the Internet and

telecommunications that available to you.

E. *Track Previous Buyers*
  1) Make a list of all previous buyers.
  2) List what area they bought in.
  3) These are proven buyers who take action and have made the move toward buying.

F. *TV*
  1) Investigate cost of commercials in your local area.
  2) It can be expensive but worth it, depending on your individual goals.

G. *Street Signs*
  1) In investor areas ("we buy houses for cash" is a good example).
  2) Try to at least place signs on your properties.

H. *Attend all Investor Club meetings*
  1) Hand out cards/list.
  2) Find out about all meetings.
  3) Attend all meetings.

I. *Signs on Property*
  1) Put "For Sale" sign on property as soon as we purchase property.

Lead Sheet

These are used to track people you speak to who may become buyers, renters, or sellers. As discussed previously, you need to get the most mileage out of every lead; these leads cost time and money. The form will help keep you organized and ensure superior follow-up on every lead. Further, treat these leads as valuable items: each cost you money, and wasting or throwing a lead away needlessly may be like throwing away a $20, $100, or even—if a lead may have been converted into a sale—a $10,000 dollar bill.

This is what works for me: paper forms that I use to track leads. For you, a computer-based lead tracking system or another type of system may work best. As you know, you need to start selling a property the moment you have it under contract; being able to properly follow up and track your buyers will increase your chances sooner than later.

In order to properly follow up with every single potential buyer, I use the following system:

I use a hardcover three-ring binder, with a 31-day monthly tab system; investors I intend to call that month are listed by the day I intend to call them. Whenever I put a new property under contract, I use this binder to choose potential buyers I want to contact in hopes of selling them my newly "acquired" property. The binder tracks my follow-up call, and I'm not leaving any of this to memory. After a short while of doing this, you are also going to be able to learn your buyers and what they are looking for. In many instances, while I am looking at a possible property to purchase I already picture who may be interested in that particular property. In essence, I identify who may be my buyer before I even put an offer on the property. Another good example is if you develop a good relationship and an understanding of your buyers. So, before you even put a property under contract to purchase, you can make a few calls and perhaps get commitment from a buyer before you even put a contract on the property you are trying to buy. Wouldn't that be great? Now, that will happen only if you have a good understanding of your buyer and a good relationship. Also, you must properly follow up and organize yourself, and that will only increase your chances to accomplish this.

Lead Sheet

Name____

Company Name______________________________________
Phone__________________________
Cell____________________________
Fax_____________________________
Email____
Buy/Sell Buy/Rent
Area____

Type SF THW Condo Multi Family Commercial
–Office/ warehouse/
Type of payment Cash / MTG

Assignment of Contract

This form is for assigning your purchase contract position to someone else, usually for a fee; we refer to this as wholesaling. For example, if you have a contract to purchase a property for $100,000 and your contract is assignable, and you find a buyer willing to pay you $110,000, you can in turn assign your position to the new buyer. Your buyer will be the one who actually closes on the subject property, while you will receive a $10,000 "assignment fee."

AGREEMENT FOR ASSIGNMENT OF CONTRACT

THIS AGREEMENT FOR ASSIGNMENT OF CONTRACT (the "Agreement") is made and entered into as of the _________ day of _________________, 20______, by and between (hereinafter referred to as "Assignor"), and _______________________ (hereinafter referred to as "Assignee"), with a mailing address of _______________________ ____________________________

WITNESSETH:
WHEREAS, Assignor, as "Buyer," entered into that certain Contract For Sale and Purchase (the "Contract") with as "Seller," a copy of which is attached hereto as Exhibit "A," for property with a physical address of ____ ________ (the "Property") and
WHEREAS, Assignee desires to purchase the Property for a purchase price of $_________________________ (the "Purchase Price") in accordance with the terms and conditions of the Contract, and WHEREAS, Assignor desires to assign all of its rights, title and interest under the Contract to Assignee as hereinafter set forth.

NOW, THEREFORE, in the consideration of the sum of TEN AND NO/100 DOLLARS ($10.00), the mutual covenants contained herein and other good and valuable consideration, the receipt and sufficiency of which is hereby acknowledged, Assignor and Assignee hereby agree as follows:

A. The above recitals are true and correct, including the recital of consideration.

B. Upon the execution of this Agreement by Assignee and Assignor, Assignee shall give to ____________________ ____ the sum of $____________________________, which amount shall be considered an earnest money deposit (the "Deposit") hereunder toward the assignment fee, in the amount of $_________________ - $_________________ = the "Assignment Fee" to be paid by Assignee to Assignor as consideration for the assignment of the Contract set forth herein. At the closing of the Property pursuant to the Contract (the "Closing"), the original deposit paid by Assignor under the terms of the Contract shall be reimbursed by Assignee to Assignor. If Assignee fails to close as provided herein and under the Contract, Assignor shall have the right, in its sole discretion, to terminate this Agreement and to retain the Deposit as agreed upon liquidated damages hereunder, whereupon the parties shall have no further obligations hereunder.

C. Upon payment by Assignee at Closing of the Purchase Price and the Assignment Fee, as well as the reimbursement of the original deposit to Assignor, Assignor shall deliver to Assignee or Assignee's agent an absolute assignment of contract (including all rights and benefits of the buyer there under).

D. Notwithstanding anything to the contrary contained herein the closing date under the Contract shall be held on or before ________________________________
, 20______________.

E. Assignee hereby agrees, in writing to assume and to be bound by, all duties and obligations of the Buyer under the Contract, including but not limited to, the payment of the Purchase Price and the payment of all closing costs to be borne by Buyer under the Contract.

F. Assignee hereby acknowledges and agrees that _______ ____ shall act as settlement/title agent for the transaction completed by the Contract, and Assignee hereby agrees to pay all sums, including but not limited to, closing agent fees, title insurance premiums, title examination fees, title search fees, and any other miscellaneous expenses incurred by the settlement/title agent for the purchase transaction contemplated by the Contract and this Agreement.

G. Assignee hereby acknowledges that Assignor is not in physical possession of the Property, has made no inspections thereof, and cannot and will not warrant the physical condition or any other matter regarding the Property, including but not limited to, the merchantability or marketability of the Property or its use for any particular purpose. In this regard, the assignment to be made by this Agreement is without recourse to Assignor, and, as between Assignor and Assignee, the sale of the Property is "As-Is, Where Is."

H. This Agreement shall be binding upon the heirs, successors, and assigns of the parties hereto, and this Agreement shall be construed in accordance with the laws of the state of . As to all matters hereunder, time is of the essence.

IN WITNESS WHEREOF, the parties have executed this Agreement as of the day and year first above written.

ASSIGNOR:______________________________

ASSIGNEE:______________________________

Guidelines for Wholesaling:

This form is used when you are trying to wholesale a property. Try to give your potential buyer/investor a 30% discount between the market value and your sales price. Good curb appeal should be a plus (helps marketability); 30 or more days to close (don't want to have to find a buyer in a week) and getting as much time as possible for marketing your property as long as possible will also help.

Guidelines for Wholesaling a Property to Another Investor

1\. Try to have 30 or more days to close in order to give yourself as much time to market as possible.
1\. Try to give your buyer at least 25% to 30% spread between the market value and your selling price.
1\. Try to list how much work a property needs.
2\. The more information you give about the property, the better. Also, the more clearly you present the information, the better.
1\. Curb appeal is a plus.

Tax Record Example:

This is not as much a form as it is a way to get you to familiarize yourself with the ever-important tax record. This is very important to understand. Keep in mind that different jurisdictions may have different formats, but ultimately they are all the same. A tax record helps you determine market value as well as basic property information. Real estate information such as sales price, sq. feet, lot size, owners information, etc. is all public information. Since the Internet is the greatest invention since white bread, instead of going to your local court house to get this info you can now get it online. I will highlight the most important part of a tax record:

Owner Information:
Owner Name: It's always good to know who owns the property. Whether it's bank owned or privately owned.

Location Information:
Legal Description: The lot and block to make sure the address matches.
County: Folio number: a good example of this is; it's like the social security number of the property

Owner Transfer Information: Deed Type:
Recording/Sale Date: / 1st Mtg Document #:
Sale Price: What price the current owner paid and when he or she purchased the property. This helps you when you are making an offer.
Last Market Sale Information:
Recording/Sale Date: When was this property sold.
Sale Price: What was the last sale of the property.

Property Characteristics:
Construction: What is the home made out of?
Living Area: How big is the home under roof
Bedrooms: How many bedroom existence in the home
Bath: How many bathroom the home has
Year Built: What year the home was built. Construction type- building type. Sometimes the home is older and there could have been an upgrade to the structure so physical inspection can reveal otherwise.
Site Information:

Zoning: What is the zoning of the home.
Lot Area: The lot size of the land that the home is setting on.
Tax Information:
Property Tax: the actual taxes for the property
Total Taxable Value: what is the value that the government puts on the home. You pay a percentage of this value for your real estate taxes.

Keep in mind that the above are all pieces of a puzzle to help you analyze the property. When you are looking to determine the ever-important market value, analyzing the comparables and making sure they are similar to your subject property in the above areas is the key to comparing apples to apples.

This form will help you get the most out of a tax record analysis. (Keep in mind that sometimes the tax record is only as good as the person entered it so it can have errors.) You can back up the information by looking at the property physically.

Violations and Liens Form

VIOLATION

When there is something wrong with the property from a legal perspective and the city has given a citation that is recorded in the public records. Keep in mind that we are looking for distressed properties, and most properties have some type of violations that exists on them. Most of the renovation that you will undertake will usually cure most of the violations, such as high grass, building needs paint, etc.

-When signing a contract to purchase a property, MAKE SURE THERE ARE NO VIOLATIONS & DON'T SIGN ANY ADDENDUM THAT WAIVES your rights TO BUY THE PROPERTY WITH VIOLATIONS.

-Before signing a contract, ask your Realtor or the seller if there are any violations on the property. Licensed professionals have the responsibility to disclose anything they know about the property that may affect you.

LIEN

When there are outstanding moneys owed associated with the property, either to a government body or a private entity. These moneys owed will be recorded in the public records.

-Make sure when signing a contract to purchase a property, THE SELLER WILL PAY FOR ALL LIENS.

-Before signing a contract, ask your Realtor or the seller if there are any liens on the property. Brokers have the professional responsibility to disclose to you if there are any liens.

The following form defines various property violations and liens that you may encounter and describes how to be aware of potential issues and avoid them. Keep in mind you can work hard to find a good investment property and work hard to put it under contract only to find out when the title company does its search that there are title issues. That is not the end of the world. As long as you familiarize yourself with how your local government works and don't sign anything you don't understand, you should stay out of trouble.

Buy, Manage, and Sell Checklists

When you find a property to purchase, these forms are a good start to make sure that you are organized and make sure you don't miss anything important that can hurt you later. I created these forms from trial and error over many deals. These forms help me stay on top of my business.

Buy Checklist

Once you have a property under contract, you will want to follow the Buy Checklist below.

INVESTOR PROJECT CHECKLIST

Date ____

Investor ____

address ____

Seller ____

Legal Description __________________________________

Buying Property

☐ Buyer: ____

☐ Seller: ______________________________

Phone #: ______________________________
Fax #: ________________________________
Contact information for seller? ______________________
Phone # ____________________________ Ext. _________
Fax # ______________________________________

☐ Contract executed by seller/buyer (you want to make sure the contract is valid and in effect).

Escrow letter / deposit: Amount $ ____________________ Date: ______/______/______ Received: _____/______/______

☐ What is the deadline on contract? ____________________________
Purchase Price $________ ____________________________
☐ Add property to closing date list.
☐ Place property on list to sell immediately, plus implement all other marketing strategies.(start the selling process)
☐ Add property to website (if applicable) (The Internet is a great marketing tool.).
☐ Send Closing Statement(HUD) to Accountant.
☐ Get a before picture of house and put it in the database (good for financing after the renovation).
☐ Check if property may be listed in the MLS.
[ ] Yes [ ] No
☐ Establish contact with the Title Company. ____________________

____

Closing agent____
Phone # ____________________________________Ext.______________
Fax # ____
adress:____

____
☐ Lender ____
Loan Amount $____________________________@_____% (know how much money you will need to do the deal)
adress:____
Person preparing docs: ______________________________
Phone #: __________________________ Fax #______________________
☐ Send Title Company the Mortgagee Clause.
☐ Insurance Company ____________________________
Paid: $ ______________
Eff. / Exp. Date: ____________________________
☐ Send a copy of Insurance Certificate to Lender.
☐ Send a copy of Insurance Certificate to Title Company.
☐ Get Title Commitment from Title Company and Municipal Lien Search.
☐ Get HUD from Title Company for Review.
☐ Send Title Company request for Processing Fee.
☐ Get Lender documents from person who is preparing them.
☐ Send Title Company our Wiring Instructions with the closing package.
☐ Make sure [ ] Rec. Receipt [ ] Mortgage and Note [ ] Deed

are in the file [ ] Executed HUD [ ] Title Insurance(these are the document you need to leave with after you closed on the property) Make sure we receive check from Title Company.

Managing Checklist

Once you close on a piece of real estate, now it's time to manage the property until you either sell it or rent it. The following checklist can help you properly execute the day-to-day duties.

Managing Owned Properties

☐ Turn on all utilities(to make sure everything runs right and that your contractor can work and test the utilities).
☐ Eliminate all external water faucets.(You don't want someone running up your utility bill.)
☐ Install locks on all water and electric meters.
Enter property into MLS.
☐ Place a lockbox and sign at the property.
☐ Maintain property.
☐ Get a picture of the property after renovation and put it in the database.
☐ Notify if no action after 30 days of purchase.

Rental

☐ Tenant Information:
Name:____
Phone # ______________________ Cell # __________________
☐ Total Rent: $ ____________________________________
Security Deposit: $ __________________________
Section 8 Pays: $ ___________ Tenant Pays: $_______________
☐ Lease Period: _____________________________________
Beginning Date: __________/___________/__________
Ending Date: __________/___________/__________
☐ Section 8 Information:
Section 8 Officer: _______________________________________
Case Worker: ________________________________
Phone # ____________________________________ Ext. ______
Fax #______________________________________
aress:____
____
☐ Agent: ____

Company: ______________________________
Phone: ______________________________
Fax:______________________________
Cell: ______________________
☐ NOTES: ______________________________
____

Selling Checklist

Once you find a buyer, it's time to do all the necessary tasks in order to get a payday. The following are the actions you must take as a seller.

Selling Property

☐ Contract executed by seller/buyer
Sale Price: $ ______________________
☐ Escrow letter / deposit: Amount $
______________________ Date: ______/______/______
Received: ______/______/______
☐ Buyer Name ______________________

Adress______________________________
____

Phone # ______________________ Ext. __________
Fax # ______________________
☐ What is the deadline on the contract? ______________________
____
☐ Who is the contact for the buyer? ______________________
____

Phone # ______________________Ext. __________
Fax #______________________
☐ Establish contact with Title Company.
____

Name of closing agent ______________________
Phone # ______________________ Ext. __________
Fax #______________________

☐ Order Payoff and fax to Title Company.
☐ Get HUD from Title Company for review.

- [ ] Make sure all Seller's docs are received from the Title Company and put in the file.
- [ ] Remove lock box & sign from the property.
- [ ] Call insurance company to cancel the policy and get a refund.
- [ ] Remove property from List, Mortgage Payment List, MLS, and website.
- [ ] Make sure all monies received.
- [ ] Turn off all utilities (if any).

To learn more about all the skill sets involved in these types of transactions, visit my website at www.TheRoadToRealEstateWealth.com.

INDEX